LONG REINING

Wilfried Gehrmann

LONG REINING

The Basics of the Classical Training Method

Translation by Anja Cain

First published in the United States of America in 2023 by
Trafalgar Square Books
North Pomfret, Vermont

Originally published in German as *Doppellonge: Eine klassische Ausbildungsmethode*.

ISBN: 978-1-64601-174-2
Library of Congress Control Number: 2023943930

Originally created in collaboration with Hildegard Gehrmann.

German editor: Irina Ludewig
Cover design: RM Didier
German proofreading: Korrekturbüro G. und W. Kirchhoff, Büren/Brenken
Interior layout: www.ravenstein2.de
Photos:
Alois Müller, Meerbusch: pages viii, 3, 9, 19, 21, 22, 23, 26, 27 top right, 28, 29, 30, 34, 38, 40, 42, 43, 44, 45, 46, 49, 52, 54, 56, 58, 59, 60, 61, 63, 65, 71, 73, 74, 75, 80, 81, 82, 83, 84, 85, 86, 90, 92, 94, 95, 96, 97, 111, 115, 117, 119, 120, 122
Archive of Hildegard and Wilfried Gehrmann: pages 27 top left, 113, 118
Archive of the German Equestrian Federation (FN): Pages 14 bottom (© Ronald Hogrebe), 15 bottom Götz Balzer, Bergisch Gladbach: page 77. Franz Honecker, Euskirchen: pages 66, 69. Julia Rau, Zornheim: Pages 14 top, 15 top. Franz Steindl, Aachen: page 15 middle. Julia Wentscher, Düsseldorf: page 14 middle.

Illustrations: Rudolf Strecker, Beelen: pages 24, 25, 105, 108, 109, 110, 115. Cornelia Koller, Schneverdingen-Heber: pages 31, 32 (2), 62.

Printed in China
10 9 8 7 6 5 4 3 2 1

Table of Contents

Foreword

Since his youth, Wilfried Gehrmann has been an enthusiastic horseman. Throughout his entire career, he has tried hard to express his love for horses by striving for a training method that includes more praise than force.

The opinions of Xenophon—born 430 BC—who wrote, "What is achieved with force is achieved without understanding," or of Pluvinel, who wrote around 1670, "We need to strive not to upset the horse and maintain his natural grace," were guide-posts for Wilfried Gehrmann.

The long reins are a great opportunity to work with horses at every level of training in a gentle and relaxed manner, and improve harmony between horse and human.

For over 40 years, Wilfried Gehrmann has applied this classical training tool in order to train horses, supplementing their training under saddle. The many advantages of long reins and the variety of possible uses inspired him to summarize his experiences in this book. It is of the utmost importance to him, though, to clarify that long-reining serves best as an additional tool in order to reach all levels of the training scale in a correct way.

In an easy-to-understand way, supplemented by photos and drawings, this book describes the practical implementation of work on long reins, and it includes tips, suggestions, and help for training horses in all disciplines.

For all horse enthusiasts interested in long-reining, this book is an excellent addition to the existing literature.

Günther Festerling

Andiamo by Amant

Introduction

The Journey Is the Reward

The seventh point of the Ethical Guidelines for Horse Care released by the German Equestrian Federation (FN) says:

"The person who engages in athletic activities with a horse is tasked with providing an education to herself and the horse. The goal of all training is the highest possible level of harmony between horse and human."

A good opportunity to reach a high level of harmony with the horse is surely longeing.

More effective than longeing with one longe line is long-reining. The trainer has many more aids at her disposal than with the single longe line. Suppleness, submission, and collection can be developed with relatively little effort, and can be applied to both riding and driving.

Historical Background of Long-Reining

The origins of work on two lines, long-reining, can be traced back to the eighteenth century. Work on long reins developed thanks to an increasing understanding of the limitations of the work between the "pillars." This new training method made it possible to train the horse while moving forward.

In driving training, long-reining—as preparation for hitching the horse to the carriage—was indispensable early on.

It is also very interesting to observe the reactions, behavior, talent, and potential of the horse from the ground. In this sense, long-reining can be thought of as riding from the ground. Here, it becomes very clear that horses need to first understand what is asked of them.

The goal of all training is **harmonious collaboration**. Long-reining should never be an end in itself; it should be implemented with the goal of **improving performance** across the board in a gentle way.

If a rider, for whatever reason—maybe because the horse is particularly difficult, or because the rider's aids are not refined yet—takes 50 minutes to create contact and roundness in her horse, the horse will not engage his back and will brace against the rider's hand the whole time. The result will be a horse that is heavy on the forehand and develops incorrect musculature (for example, on the lower neck), which will only worsen the problem.

In general, the horse will be exposed to more strain than he would be if he were ridden correctly. If the trainer is skillful and able to supple the horse within 15 minutes on long reins, and can carry this suppleness over to work under saddle, riding will be a continuous success instead of a struggle. The rider will experience progress, improved movement, and the opportunity to move forward to the next level in the training of the horse.

In order to effectively work a horse on long reins, the trainer needs both theoretical knowledge of correct movement in the horse, and the practical skill to implement this knowledge.

Understanding the horse and progressing in **small steps—without overwhelming** the horse—using **patience** and **sensitivity, much praise**, and **occasional corrections,** are needed in the education of the horse.

It takes a lot of practice to train horses on long reins and correct "problem horses." But it's possible to ask a horse to move correctly and create suppleness with just a few exercises.

Non-riders will be able, with appropriate practice, to work horses correctly. If a horse needs to work off some excess energy, it's better to let him do it on long reins, in a controlled, productive way, than to let him charge around the arena.

Amant, a registered stallion, born in 1981 by Amazonas/Absatz, out of Libelle, by Lotse/Lugano. The author won 25 third and fourth level dressage tests on him, and attributes that not just to the horse's natural potential and talent, but also to consistent work on long reins. With that work, the author was able to create harmony without force. In addition, long-reining supported the correct development of the horse's musculature and the ability to collect. As you can see in this picture, Amant performs the piaffe following the lightest aids.

Some people, even well-known people, may say that when horses are worked on the longe or long reins often, riding skills are lacking. This statement is not true.

A skilled rider who has many aids at her disposal may not need to longe the horse in order to make him supple. This rider may not mind sitting some bucking, and may be able to provide all the necessary training from the saddle.

However, every rider is limited in some way. Looking at the variation between individual horses, their different physical and psychological potential, and problem horses and horses that need corrective work, sooner or later we all reach a point where progress seems impossible. In this situation, long-reining can be the solution—whether problems have arisen due to safety concerns, because the rider is lacking the skills to ride the horse while encouraging the horse's back to engage, or because there are specific exercises that are difficult for the horse to perform with a rider.

Long-reining needs to be done in such a way that even a critical observer can see the effectiveness of the activity.

In general, long-reining can only be considered negative if it is done by an unqualified person. The theoretical basis for long-reining is the **Training Scale,** which embodies the classical training system and is valid for longeing and long-reining as well as riding and driving.

1 Required Theoretical Knowledge

"Training can only be good and effective if it is done in a systematic way. Educating horses and improving their performance is relatively easy if you are knowledgeable about the training system you are using."

The Training Scale

The theoretical basis for the entire education of the horse, in classical equestrian theory, is called the Training Scale. This is the thread that continues through training in general and through each individual training session. It is important to know where on the Scale the horse currently is and how to implement the Scale in your daily work.

Important!
The best way to guarantee your horse's welfare is not only consistent training and development for him, but also continuing the education and training of his rider/driver, in theory and in practice.

The Training Scale is organized into six elements, with the transition between these training elements being gradual.

The common goal of the six elements: Harmony—Performance—Health

A brief definition of the six elements, according to the Guidelines of the German Equestrian Federation (FN):

1. Rhythm is spatial and temporal symmetry in the three basic gaits, referring to steps, strides, and jumps.

2. Suppleness is the engagement of the horse's musculature, devoid of any tension. Rhythmic, relaxed movement has to include an engaged back.

3. Contact is the steady, soft, supple link between the rider's hand and the horse's mouth. The FN Guidelines state: "Contact is sought by the horse and allowed by the rider."

4. Impulsion is the transmission of energy from the hindquarters through a swinging back and into the forward movement of the horse.

5. Straightness is when the forehand matches up to the hindquarters—when the horse tracks up on straight and bent lines.

6. Collection is achieved when the hindquarters take on more weight, while bending more in the hock joints and stepping even farther underneath the horse.

The Context of Systematic Training

The Training Scale

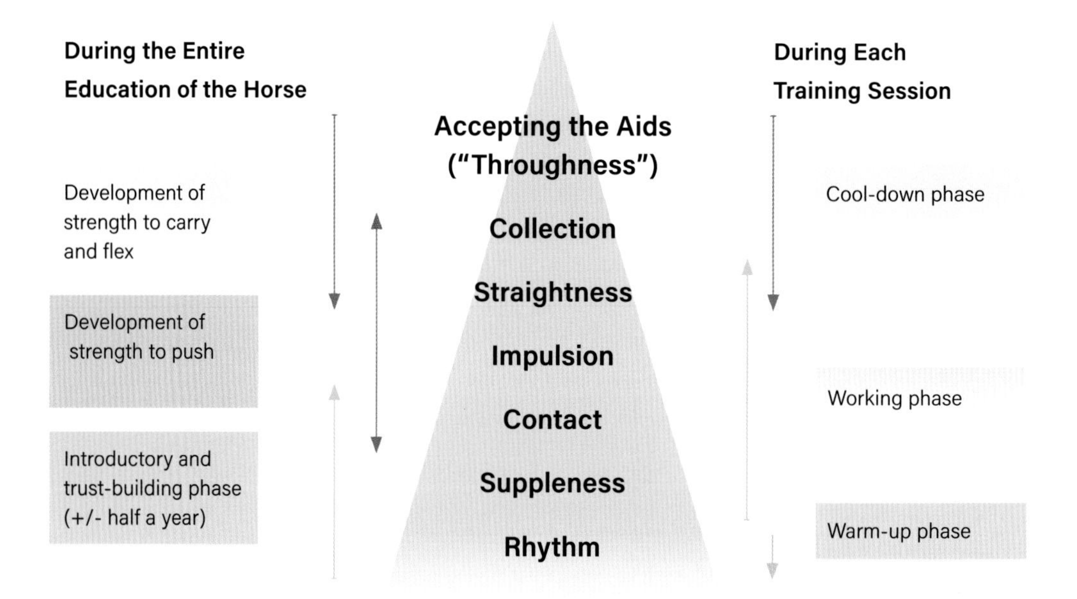

Acceptance of the aids ("thoroughness") improves with training. All elements of the training scale relate to each other (there are no strict boundaries, but rather fluid transitions between the elements).
Goal: Harmony—Performance—Health
Solid training = animal welfare

The Three Main Phases of Training

During the entire education of the horse—no matter the discipline—we are typically dealing with three main phases. The transitions between these phases are fluid, since each horse is different when it comes to talent, temperament, and character. Each trainer is different, too, in terms of her level of knowledge and skill. These factors are important for the future career of the horse.

Familiarization and Trust-Building Phase

During the introductory trust-building phase, which lasts about half a year, the focus is on familiarizing the horse with humans, equipment, longeing, and, if riding is the objective, with a rider. This includes the horse learning to accept humans as trusted authorities—without any force, using caution and care.

The goal of this introductory and trust-building phase is to produce a horse that can carry a rider while staying balanced in all three basic gaits, without tension, and with a low neck and a light connection. Once this goal is achieved, the first three elements of the training scale, **rhythm, suppleness,** and **contact**, are achieved.

Developing Strength to Push and Refining Movement

With a foundation of solid basic training—with emphasis on the trusting relationship between horse and human—the second phase of training, the development of strength to push and refinement of the horse's movement, including the elements of **impulsion** and **straightness,** can begin. This can only be successful if the first elements of the training scale have been mastered fully. Moving on too quickly will lead to unevenness, tension, and resistance, or a faulty connection.

Too little attention is often paid to the element of impulsion. Impulsion can only be developed if the horse's back is healthy.

Important!
The back is the center of the horse's movement. Every half-halt should move hind to front and front to hind over the horse's back.

The freely swinging back is a basic prerequisite for a horse to fully accept the aids. Even a rider who is more or less balanced on the horse may not always be able to activate the horse's back using her aids—and without an active, swinging back and a full connection to the aids, the horse can never reach his full potential as a riding horse.

The issue of the **natural crookedness** in each horse should be addressed early in the horse's training. Every horse is more or less crooked—most horses are slightly crooked to the right.

In order to maintain the horse's health, it is important to work **symmetrically** in both directions so the horse will accept the rider's aids equally on both sides.

In a "straightened" horse, his mass is positioned evenly in front of his hindquarters, allowing pushing strength to develop evenly likewise, and all half-halts to reach the hindquarters. This horse is on the rider's aids, and the prerequisites are present to move on to the third phase of training.

Developing Strength to Carry and Flex

During the third phase of training, pushing strength will be developed not only in a forward direction, but also forward and upward simultaneously. This allows for increased weight-bearing by the hindquarters. The strength to carry and flex is being developed. Suppleness plays a big role in allowing the horse to move in a light and cadenced way. Depending on the level of collection and the flexing of the joints in the hindquarters, the horse now moves in **relative self-carriage.**

In this frame and posture, the horse has reached his highest level of **acceptance of the aids;** this allows for **harmonious and light riding and driving,** and the horse will be able to perform for many years.

In a correctly trained four-and-a-half to five-year-old, this phase can be started.

The Three Main Phases within a Training Unit

Each training session is structured in three phases. But, again, there is no rigid boundary between these phases.

Warm-Up Phase

You must start with a warm-up in each training session. The horse should work at the walk first in order to engage him and prepare him for the work ahead. Then he should perform trot work in a controlled tempo, and after that, the canter should be included.

The appropriate warm-up exercises depend on the level of the horse's training. With horses who have had correct training—who have achieved **rhythm, suppleness,** and **contact**—this goal will be reached after 15 to 20 minutes.

A horse that is moving with rhythm and relaxation and is stretching into the contact can now start the working phase.

Planning a Training Session for a Well-Trained Horse

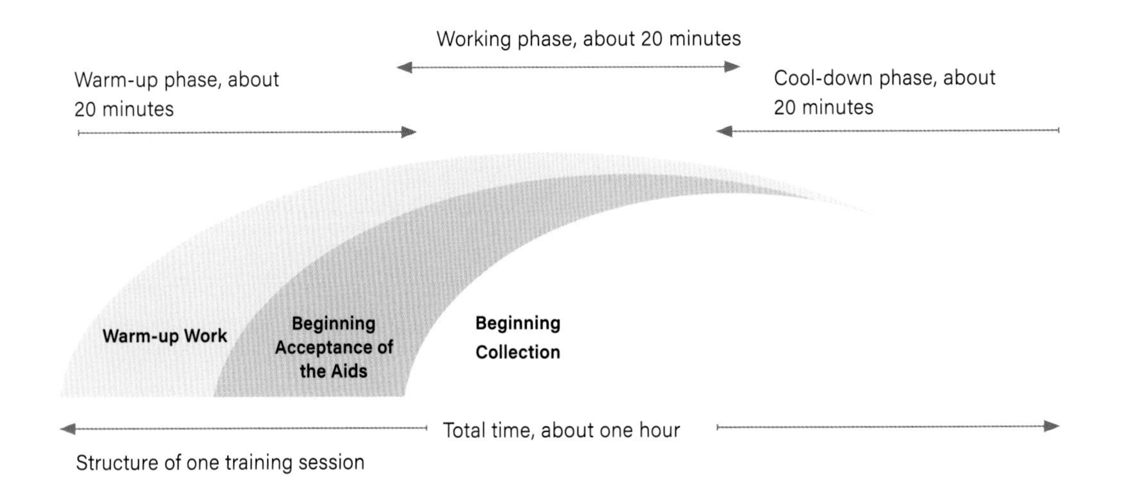

Structure of one training session

Working Phase

During the working phase, the additional elements of the Training Scale—**impulsion, straightness, and collection**—are developed, depending on the horse's level of training and discipline.

In order to avoid too much strain, this phase should not exceed 20 minutes. Should problems occur during the working phase, they cannot be solved with increasingly forceful aids. The sensitive trainer will take a few steps back, reinforce the elements of basic training, and then start again.

Cool-Down Phase

During the final cool-down phase, it is essential to ride the horse in a long-and-low frame, in order to end on a positive note and ensure good conditions for the next day.

The time estimates in the diagram on this page are for the education of the riding horse. When you're working on long reins, the individual phases are shorter, since the objectives can be reached more quickly. Additionally, working for too long on a 20-meter circle may put too much strain on the horse. Work on long reins should not exceed half an hour.

Varied and Individual

When considering training progress and the horse's health, it's best to keep the overall workload varied and individualized but also relatively consistent. Working intensively for two hours one day, and then not working at all the next day—because the horse worked so hard the day before—won't facilitate either progress in schooling or development of the horse's musculature.

General Principles

No matter what discipline a horse will be working in, specific rules need to be followed.

As a general rule, the entire education of a horse must progress in **small steps**. The expectations a trainer has for a horse should not be forced or rushed. Otherwise, physical and psychological problems can occur that are very difficult to correct later.

Understand and implement the principle of moving from **easy** exercises to **difficult** exercises, and you'll see steady progress. Plateaus and regressions are absolutely normal; the causes are mostly developmental, and will even out on their own.

If the horse's basic training has been solid, a trainer can always fall back on it when problems arise.

It is absolutely wrong to use forceful aids and overwork the horse, or use draw reins and harsh bits to demand unrealistic success.

Important!
Next to the technical skills needed to train a horse, the acknowledgment of the horse as an individual and the creation of a trusting relationship are paramount for a harmonious give-and-take and success under saddle.

The prudent trainer needs to ask herself whether a horse who is resistant doesn't **want** to do the exercise, or **can't.** It would be too easy to only look at challenges from a technical point of view, and say, "He just needs to push through."

It is just as important to investigate the causes of setbacks, so they can be addressed, as it is to investigate the causes for success, so it can be repeated. This requires a holistic view of the horse. Conformation, temperament, talent, conditions, and, first and foremost, level of training are factors that need to be taken into consideration.

When problems surface, it is imperative to make sure the horse is not suffering from any health problems, and that pain is not the reason he is resisting the aids.

If the trainer has sufficient skills and sticks to the classical system of training, success will come with competence.

A horse's education can only be successful and effective if it is approached in a systematic way. Training horses and developing them to perform better is relatively straightforward, if you are knowledgeable about this training system.

2 Variety of Applications of Long Reins

The applications of long reins are widely varied. The discipline a horse is trained for, the level of training the horse has reached, and whether the horse is trained for pleasure riding or competition—none of these things limit the potential value of long reins.

Generally speaking, there are no major differences between disciplines when it comes to what constitutes correct movement of the horse. We are looking for correct dynamic movements, natural self-carriage, and a harmonic overall impression.

If the benefits of working with long reins can be realized, long-reining can be successfully used in training for **all equestrian disciplines.**

Variety in Training

All horses should be worked in a way that is varied and versatile. This is not just beneficial for the rider—it also helps maintain the horse's **well-being** and **health**. Every horse should get basic training in all disciplines.

It would be wrong, for example, to only work on dressage exercises with a dressage horse. The horse may perform the exercises successfully, but without radiance, joy in his movements, motivation, or lightness.

The horse's motivation can be maintained with **regular trail rides**, and his suppleness can be encouraged by **working over ground poles** and **gymnastic jumping**.

Long-reining is one more way to motivate the horse.

The horse should also have the opportunity to move freely, by giving him access to pasture.

Varied Implementations of Long-Reining . . .

... in dressage.

... in pole work.

... for the eventing horse.

... for the jumper.

... for the driving horse.

... for the vaulting horse.

During the Introduction and Trust-Building Phase

It is possible to work even young horses, during the introduction and trust-building phase, on long reins. They get accustomed to the equipment and grow familiar with the two-sided attachment of the long reins, which resembles the future sensations of rein aids. While moving on a 20-meter circle, young horses will learn to find their natural balance. The training goal for young horses is rhythm and relaxation while stretching forward and downward.

When horses have been trained in this way, they provide more control and safety for the rider or driver. They typically move without any problems from the get-go.

For Warming Up

In addition to ongoing basic training, long reins can be used to warm up the horse. This supports an **active back**, without interference from the rider's weight.

During Advanced Training

The acceptance of the aids in a state of lightness (*Durchlässigkeit*) is improved during advanced training—in particular, by practicing transitions on the long reins. Here, we are looking for natural self-carriage in the horse. Exercises that present challenges for the rider or driver can be addressed with very little effort on the long reins.

At this point, the education of the horse focuses on rhythm, relaxation, and contact. In addition, long-reining improves impulsion and, by asking the horse to practice consistent bend, it also improves straightness.

Work Over Ground Poles for All Horses

In the interest of a varied education, working over ground poles, raised ground poles, and jumps for gymnastic purposes on long reins offers many advantages.

For the Jumper

In addition to jumping under saddle and free jumping, long reins offer one more opportunity to work on jumping. Leg technique, bascule, and control can be improved.

For the Driving Horse

For the driving horse, long-reining is nothing less than necessary. This work familiarizes the horse with lines and reins, and he learns to react appropriately to cues from the voice and whip. Only a carefully trained horse will offer the safety, control, and acceptance necessary to participate in driving as a sport.

For the Vaulting Horse

Long reins can be a helpful and appropriate addition to the training, correction, and exercise of the vaulting horse. For horses who are not being ridden in a qualified way, long-reining can function as a balance to the work of equestrian vaulting. In this sense, it helps maintain the **horse's health**.

For the Advancement of the Dressage Horse

During the education of the advanced level dressage horse, development of collection with the help of long reins is entirely possible. On the single longe line, this is only possible for very skilled trainers.

Working on collection is possible on long reins.

For Corrective Work

For corrective work in particular, long reins have proven to be very effective. With every single problem that shows up, it is important for the horse to revisit the basic elements of the Training Scale—rhythm and relaxation—in order to build on those basics.

3 Education of the Trainer

In order to be effective, the trainer needs to have deep knowledge of the correct way of moving for a horse and the practical skills to shape the horse toward the desired frame and posture.

Requirements

When working with long reins, it is imperative to avoid difficult and dangerous situations by first mastering the technique of longeing. As long as the trainer still struggles to manage the long reins and the whip, the horse cannot be expected to react correctly to the aids

Important!
For safety reasons, it is recommended to start out working under the supervision of a trainer who's experienced with long reins.

It is highly recommended to start off working with an experienced horse. He will forgive your mistakes and will not react by panicking. Older, experienced long-reining horses and geldings who are not very sensitive are best suited for a beginner to long-reining.

It is always recommended to wear gloves—not only when starting out with the first exercises, but at all times when long-reining. The gloves should be grippy to keep the long reins from sliding through your hands.

Do not wear spurs when long-reining. No matter how careful you are, the long reins might get caught on the spur and cause you to trip and fall.

The Aids

Similar to riding, success in long-reining is dependent on correct interactions between the aids. The trainer has the following aids at her disposal: voice, whip, and long reins.

Normal longeing with the help of a more experienced trainer.

First change of direction.

The experienced trainer supervises long-reining . . .

. . . and explains how to proceed through the change of direction.

Voice

The voice can have the effect of pushing the horse forward or slowing him down. Higher-pitched, shorter, brisker voice commands have a forward-pushing effect, while lower-pitched, quieter sounds have a calming effect. Through the repetition of specific words, horses will learn to remember them as signals and will demonstrate appropriate reactions. For example, a calming "halt" for a full halt, and an energetic "canter" for a canter depart. The voice is an essential aid for long-reining, and at the same time should be kept to a minimum—it is only to influence the horse working on the long reins, and not other horses present in the arena.

The Whip

Generally, a horse is not supposed to **be afraid** of the whip, but rather to show **respect for it.** It will be necessary for the trainer to be able to touch the horse anywhere on his body, with different levels of intensity. Only then can the whip be used effectively to **increase tempo and energy** and **move the horse outward.**

It is helpful to practice handling the whip without a horse.

The Long Reins

The aids applied with long reins are similar to rein aids. The trainer needs to be able to influence the horse with feel in every situation, using specific techniques. As when riding, the contact should be light, confident, and consistent. Ideally, the trainer only carries the weight of the long reins in her hands. When it comes to how to hold the long reins, there is no exact rule. The deciding factor is the quality of the horse's movement. Specific holds and techniques have been proven to work well to lead the horse with little effort.

Two-Handed Hold

When long-reining young, strong horses, a two-handed hold is recommended. The long reins will run—in both hands—between the little finger and the ring finger, similar to holding ordinary reins in a closed hand. A two-handed hold will also be necessary when working on transitions and specific exercises like a full halt.

When progressing in training, generally the long reins should be held in one hand, since this supports a more consistent and stable connection.

One-Handed Hold

When long-reining to the left, a one-handed hold means the left long rein runs between the thumb and pointer finger, and the right long rein between the ring and middle finger of the left hand. The excess at the end of the long rein can run over the little finger. This way, one hand can be used to position the horse to the inside or outside, by turning the hand. In addition, the wrist or the arm can be used for shortening and lengthening.

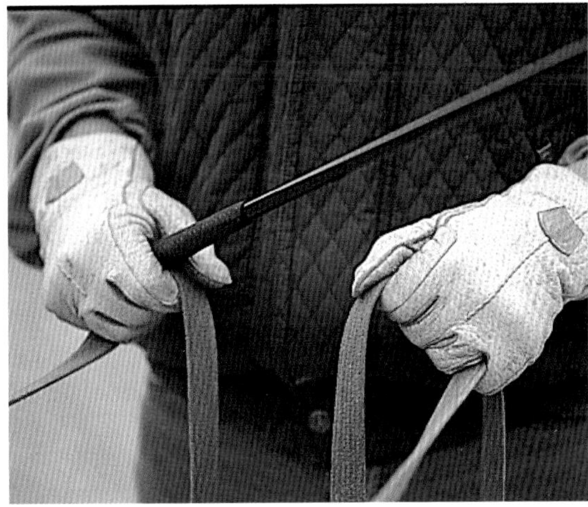

Two-handed hold of the long rein to the right.

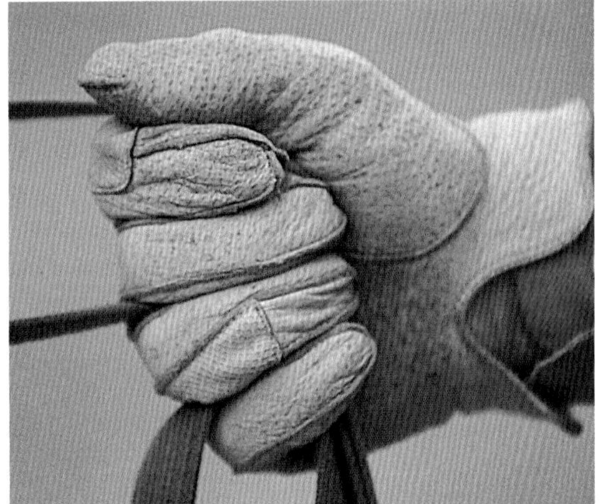

One-handed hold of the long rein to the right.

After a change of direction, the long reins and whip need to be switched to create a mirror image. Of course, a variety of holds are possible. It is most important for the trainer to be safe and effective in influencing the horse.

Combining the Aids

Correct long-reining of the horse depends first and foremost on the activity of the haunches and correct interactions between the aids. When riding, the seat, leg, and rein aids need to work together with feel. The same interaction between the aids exists in long-reining. The voice aids can be compared to the seat aids, which can be applied in order to push forward or slow down. The whip replaces the leg aids, and the long reins are, of course, analogous to ordinary reins.

In order to put a horse in a particular frame, the trainer has to practice half-halts. Here, the horse is first activated with the forward-pushing aids, toward a steady contact. As soon as the trainer sees and feels that the horse is releasing the poll and accepting the aids, she needs to immediately get light in her hands and give with the long reins. This will prevent the horse from becoming "stuck" or tense.

One-handed hold, going to the left. The long rein is held in the inside hand, and the whip is in the outside hand, pointed toward the croup.

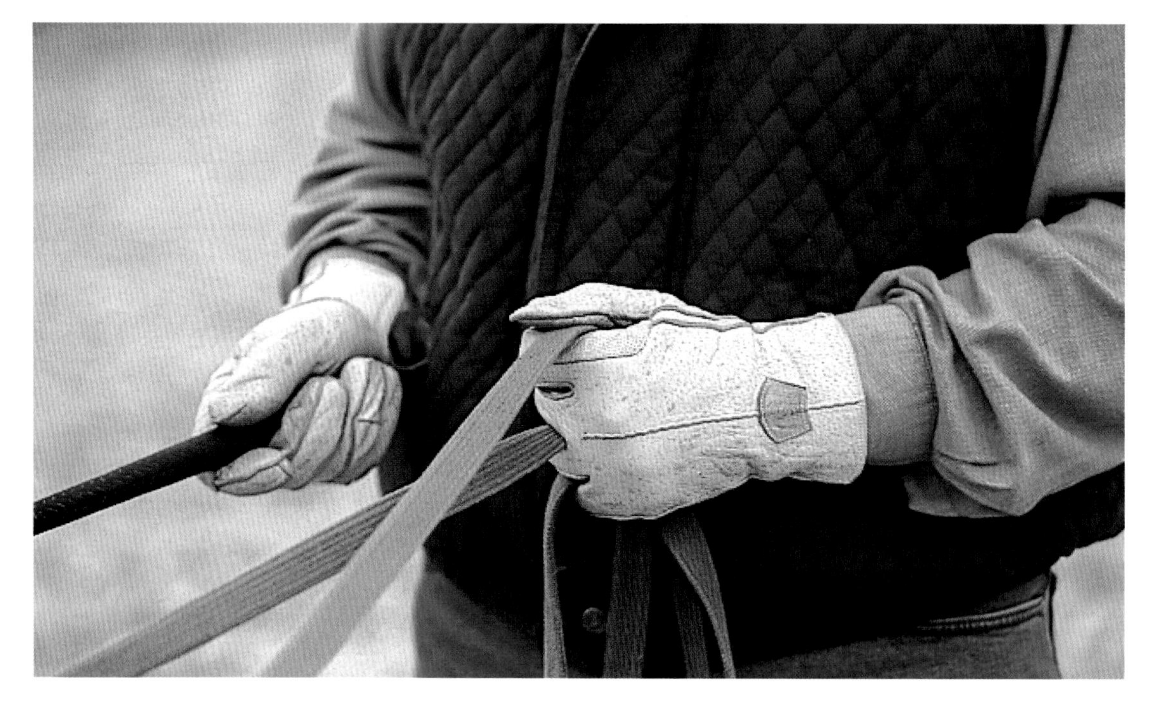

The trainer demonstrates the shortening and lengthening of the inside long rein.

If the trainer wants to improve positioning and bend, she needs to point the whip toward the shoulder to move the horse outward, and simultaneously turn the inside hand to shorten the long rein in order to position the horse. Here, too, an immediate release of the inside long rein is paramount. On the one hand, this prevents the horse from falling out over the outside shoulder, and on the other hand, the connection stays light.

Important!
Success in long-reining depends on steadying the hindquarters and giving or lengthening the long rein in the right moment, with feel.

Change of Direction

Changes of direction can be daunting at first. To change direction from one circle to another or through one circle, with correct position and bend and in the desired tempo, requires skill, feel, and a lot of practice.

Change of Direction Through One Circle

In order to change direction through one circle, the length of the long reins remains the same and the trainer moves toward the outer track of the circle—this results in the horse moving toward the center of the circle. When reaching the track, the new outside long rein should be lengthened, and the new inside long rein should be shortened. Then the trainer moves back toward the center of the circle and guides the horse outward to the track. In the new direction, the long reins must be organized, and the horse positioned on the line of travel. During the change of direction, the whip needs to be managed skillfully.

Change of direction through one circle.

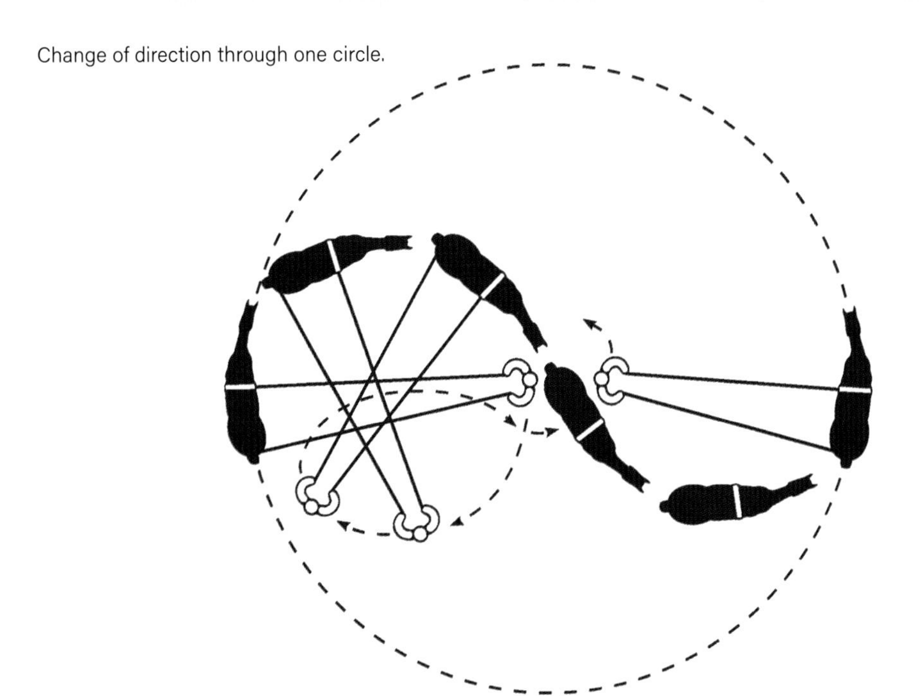

Change of Direction from One Circle to Another

To change direction from one circle to another, the trainer repositions the horse when crossing the centerline. To achieve this, she lengthens the outside long rein as much as she shortens the inside long rein, while moving along the centerline to the center of the new circle. Many trainers have the tendency to walk with the horse—they don't stay in one place. When working with young horses, it may be necessary to walk with them most of the time, but if the goal is for the horse to work in the correct bend, and straightness is to improve, it is necessary for the trainer to stay in one place, to ensure the horse is being worked on a correct line for the circle.

Even though these first exercises and the change of direction on long reins may seem complicated, with practice and routine, it will be possible to work horses effectively.

Change of direction from one circle to another.

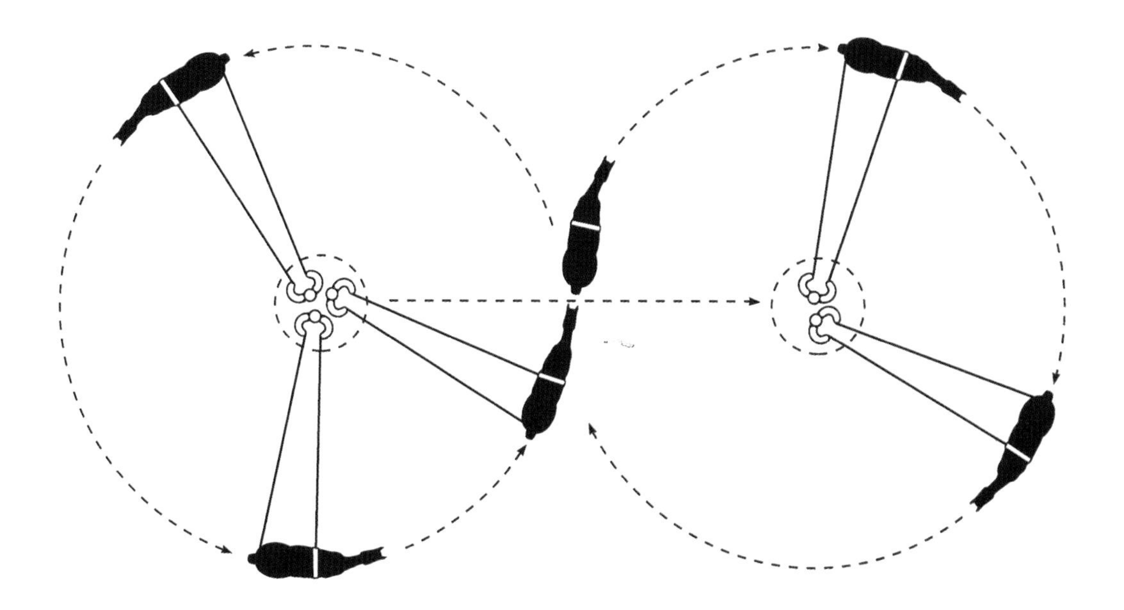

4 Equipment

An essential requirement for correct long-reining is the appropriate equipment. Assuming the horse is working in a bitted bridle, the following pieces of equipment are needed.

The Long Reins

The long reins—they are one piece—should be 16 to 18 meters (50 to 60 feet) long. This allows for young horses to be worked on long reins on a larger circle. The material should not be slippery, and should be comfortable for the hands.

Long reins with rollers.

Shorter, thinner long reins, particularly appropriate for long-reining.

Thick white cotton long reins—comfortable for the hands, but without elasticity, and, because of their thickness, only appropriate for large hands.

Thick, robust nylon long reins—very sturdy, but slick, and may slide through the hands if horses are strong and like to pull.

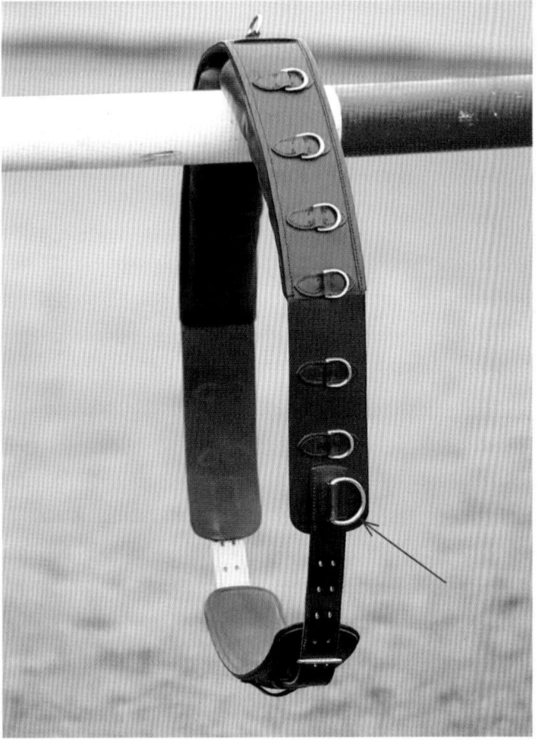

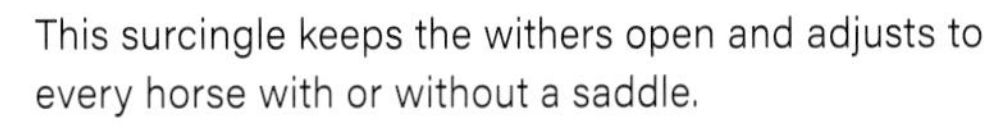

This surcingle keeps the withers open and adjusts to every horse with or without a saddle.

The long-reining surcingle: The many rings allow the trainer to adjust the height at which the long reins attach. The lowest ring needs to be large enough to allow the clips or buckles of the rein to fit through it. A surcingle can be used over a saddle or directly on the horse.

Saddle and Surcingle

Depending on the training goals, the horse will be worked in a surcingle, with or without a saddle. If you are using a surcingle by itself, make sure you use correct padding. The rings on the surcingle need to be placed low enough, and they need to be large enough. This is not the case on some surcingles so be cautious when making your selection.

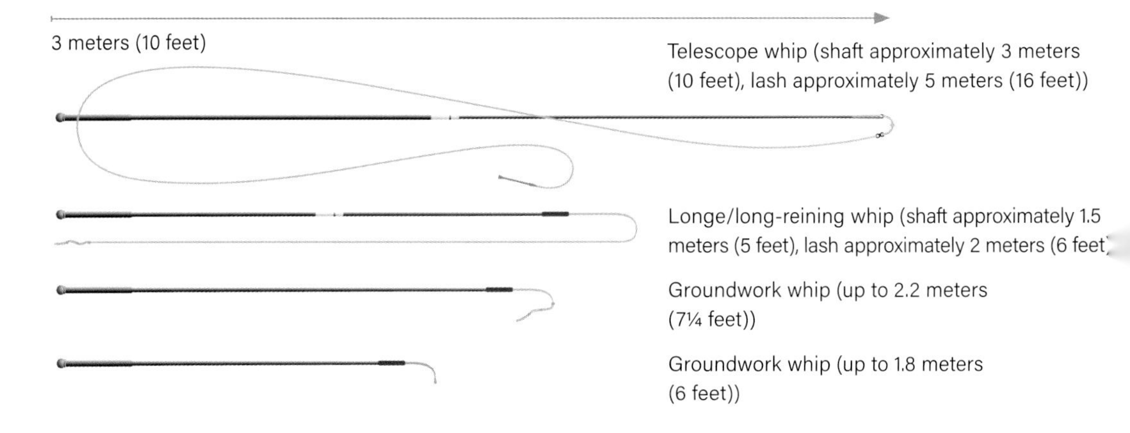

Whip

The length of the whip you should use depends on the sensitivity of the horse. Normally, a whip should be long enough—approximately 7 to 8 meters (20 to 25 feet), including the lash—to reach the horse anywhere on his body.

Carabiners or Rings

In order to attach the long reins to the saddle—for example, to the girth—you will need carabiners, or ring loops for short dressage girths.

Attaching a carabiner to the girth.

Ring loop for short girths.

Attaching the ring loop to a short girth.

Leg Protection

The legs of the horse should always be protected with boots or wraps when working on long reins.

If the goal is to achieve relaxation before riding, and the horse is being long-reined for 15 minutes, the horse should be tacked up with a saddle and bridle.

When attaching the long reins at the height shown in the photo below, it's possible for the horse to be too short in the neck after the warm-up phase. In order to allow the horse to regain his natural self-carriage, the long reins need to be attached higher. When working on collection, the position of the reins needs to allow the horse to move in self-carriage.

The horse is tacked up to be ridden directly after work on the long reins. For long-reining, the riding reins have been secured by the throatlatch, and the stirrups have been securely wrapped. The horse is wearing wraps on all four legs for protection. To work toward suppleness and relaxation, the long reins should be attached in a way that creates a horizontal connection between the bit and the girth.

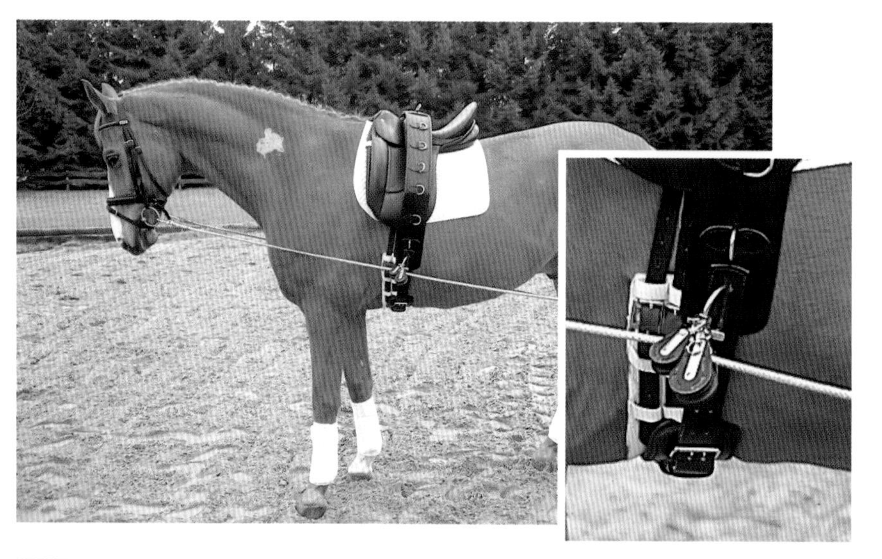

The rein is attached as low as possible on the surcingle with the addition of a "roller." This position is particularly appropriate for working toward suppleness and relaxation during the warm-up phase, and also providing a long-and-low frame for the cool-down phase.

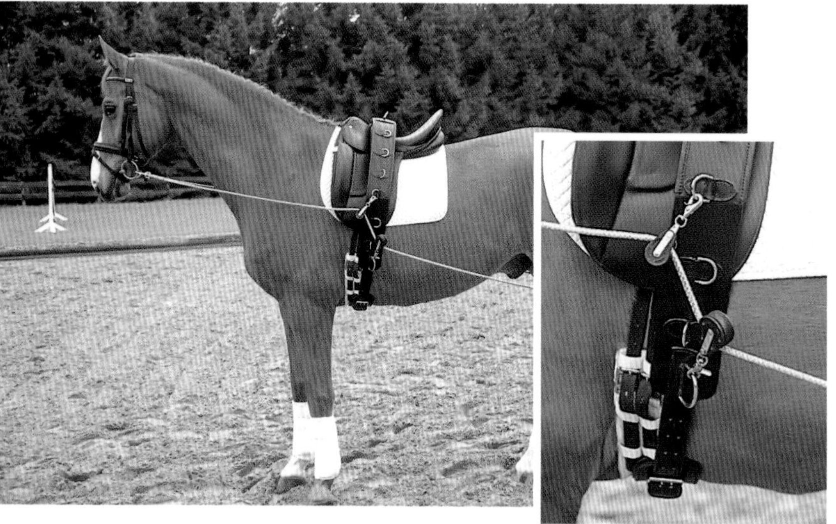

Attaching the reins at medium height can be helpful when a warmed-up horse is too short in the neck and needs to be guided toward self-carriage.

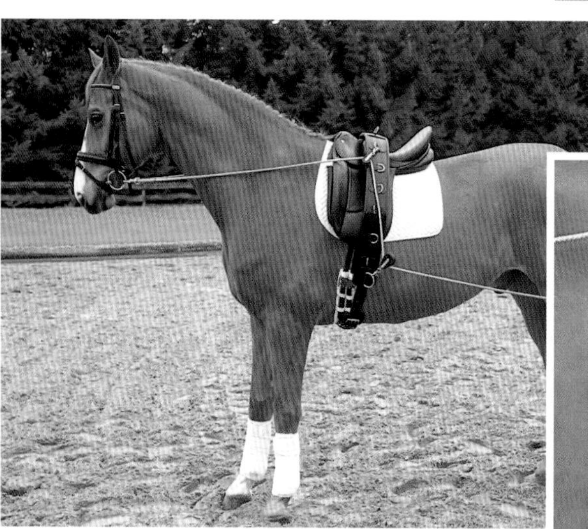

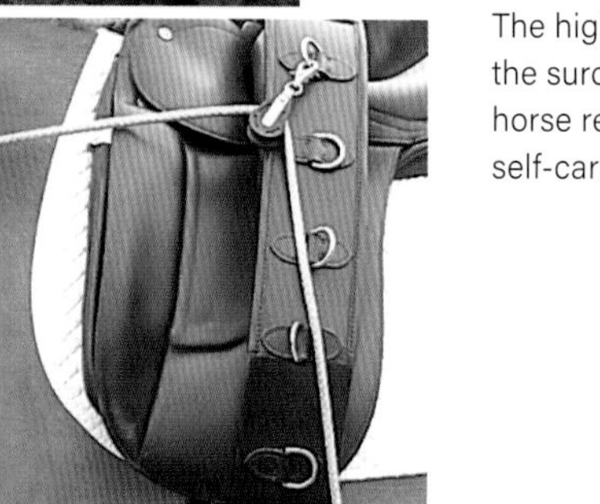

The highest position on the surcingle asks that a horse reach correct self-carriage.

The long reins can be used with a surcingle for this purpose. Different positions on the surcingle can be adopted depending on the horse's training goals.

Redirecting long reins with the use of a "roller" mechanism, as shown in the photographs, can prevent the frictional resistance that can hinder the effectiveness of the aids—in particular, a quick and gentle give with the long reins is difficult. Long reins can also be used as a support, or a correctional rein. This approach works when longeing or long-reining. The effect on the horse is similar to that of Lauffer reins. Lauffer reins are attached as a sideways triangle. The different ways of attaching the long reins—described in the following text—require a lot of practice on the part of the trainer. The horse getting short in the neck or falling out over his shoulder should be avoided. Coordination of the aids and a sensible, slow approach to finding the correct height of attachment of the long reins are crucial for the success of this work.

A narrow, low-set triangle supports give in the poll, control, and willingness to stretch, and therefore creates suppleness and relaxation.

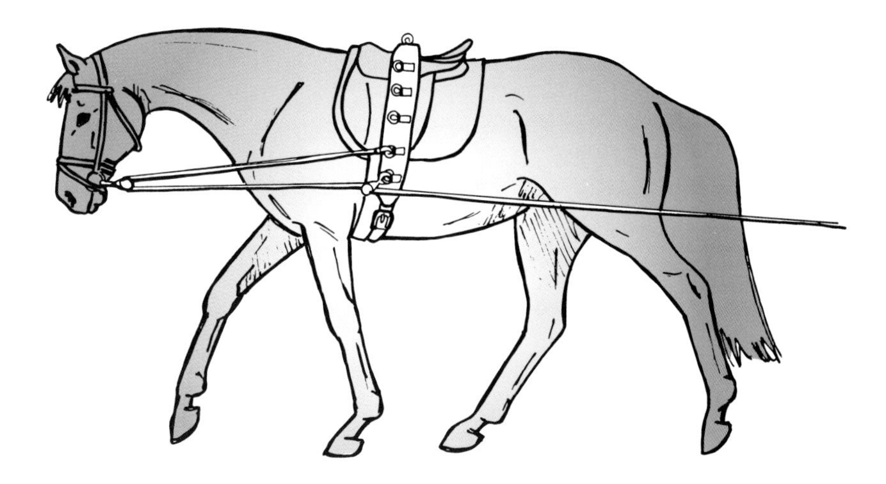

For this attachment, the long reins run from the surcingle to the bit and back to the surcingle.

In this work, it should be the goal to manage with a single long rein.

A medium-sized triangle can improve self-carriage.

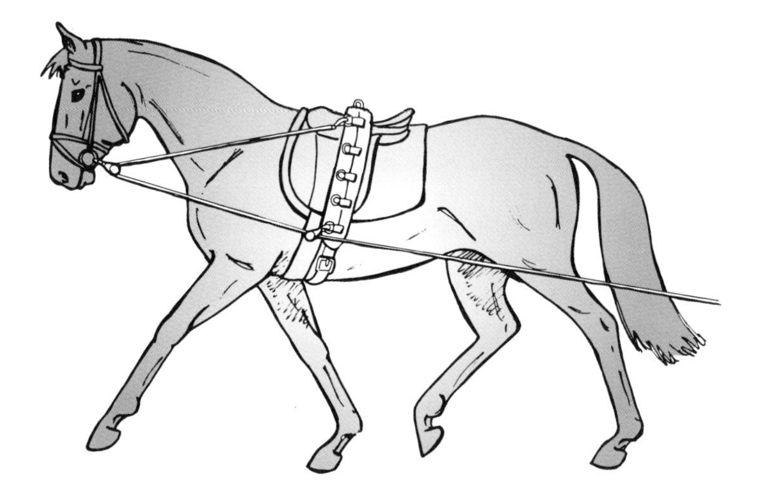

A higher-set triangle makes self-carriage possible, but understand that self-carriage is relative. This setting is particularly well-suited for strong horses. Throughout your work, typically the connection will get lighter and therefore more pleasant for both horse and trainer.

5 Preparation of the Young Horse Prior to Being Ridden

I am sure there are many proven ways to train young horses. However, even the most careful training cannot guarantee that a young horse won't show anxiety and buck or bolt when ridden for the first time. This creates a dangerous situation for the rider.

Preparing the young horse with long reins before he is ridden for the first time has many advantages.

The horse must be familiar with the single longe line, saddle, and bridle, at a minimum.

Preparing to Ride without the Use of Side-Reins

Some challenges that often occur when young horses are being longed on a single longe line can be avoided with long-reining. Often, horses will oppose any additional reins, like side-reins.

When, for example, the side-reins are set too short, or you are working with a particularly sensitive horse, it is normal for the horse to feel constricted. He may try to raise his head, panic, or rear, and in the worst case scenario, he could fall over backward.

Such an experience will not encourage a trusting relationship between horse and trainer.

On long reins, by contrast, the horse is able to raise his head. Often, raising the head is caused by a lack of balance on the circle.

This young horse clearly shows how long reins allow enough freedom for the horse to move naturally.

By giving with both reins, all resistance can be avoided. Once the horse relaxes and lowers the neck, he has the opportunity to find a soft, elastic connection. Working in a long, low frame becomes possible.

Preparation in the Three Basic Gaits

Depending on the potential of the horse, this long, low frame is only possible in the walk and trot, at first. Very few horses have better balance in the canter. A slight positioning to the outside is permissible in the beginning.

If a horse has balance challenges in the canter, those issues will typically resolve themselves once he has learned to relax in the trot. Often, horses will rush and lack regulation in their tempo at first. Once they learn to balance themselves on the circle, though, they will find rhythm in their movement by achieving a steady tempo.

Familiarization with the Aids

A horse that was prepared this way on long reins usually accepts the rider right away—naturally, caution still needs to be used, but:

- The horse is already familiar with the rein aids. He accepts the human voice in a trusting manner, too, for both forward aids and calming aids.
- The horse is not afraid of the whip, which will be replaced with a short crop when riding.
- Because the long reins touch the horse where the rider's leg will be positioned, the horse is able to accept the rider's leg more quickly.

Careful Preparation

Preparation before the first mounted work with the horse cannot be done carefully enough, since it lays the groundwork for all future training. If, for example, the girth is tightened too abruptly in the beginning, the horse may react badly to being saddled for the rest of his life.

Important!
By working slowly, you give the horse the opportunity to understand what you are asking of him and to cooperate in a manner that reflects trust, in the absence of force.

A special benefit of long reins is that the horse learns to cooperate and accept the human as someone whose requests he will try to heed. This is particularly important with horses that have a strong personality, and especially with stallions, who naturally strive to put themselves in charge. Peaceful cooperation should happen early, and should be encouraged with patience to ensure ongoing partnership.

Time—No "Cookie Cutter Approach"

How much time is needed to prepare for a horse's first mounted work cannot be stated as a rule. It depends on a horse's talent, temperament, and potential, and the skill of his trainer. When a horse has plenty of contact with humans during his first years growing up, and has developed trust as a result, this phase can be relatively short. Typically, this phase will be about one month long, but that is only a general estimate.

Challenges for the Trainer

Long-reining a horse needs to be done very carefully, the first time. The age of the horse doesn't matter. Older horses who are used to being ridden need the same level of diligence here as young horses.

As a rule, horses with no prior experience with long reins need to be introduced to this work by trainers with a lot of **experience**.

We always have to proceed under the assumption that horses can only learn when their nerves are steady. Where fear and panic reign, progress is impossible. You can build on a horse's intelligence, but you should never assume you can control his instinctive behavior.

It is the horse's nature to react to fear by bolting and fleeing.

The art of the trainer using long reins is to know the temperament and personality of the horse so well that she can predict his reactions and adapt her methods accordingly. Unsupervised long-reining done by an inexperienced trainer is likely to cause unnecessary accidents, and is a waste of what might have been a valuable training opportunity.

6 Long-Reining for the First Time

The very first time a horse is worked on long reins has the potential to be particularly difficult. It is paramount for all involved that the horse become familiar with this work in a safe and controlled manner, and develop trust in long-reining. The objective for young horses during this familiarization phase is mastering the first three elements of the Training Scale:

- **Rhythm**
- **Suppleness**
- **Contact**

When working with very forward horses, it is advisable to first longe them on a single line before attaching long reins, or if trained to saddle, ride them. Using this method, you can guarantee that excess energy has already been addressed.

Appropriate Long-Reining Area

A safe **longeing arena** or **longeing circle** are the most appropriate locations for using long reins for the first time. In any case, the area where you are long-reining should have secure footing, since the horse can begin to move quickly and he may go around for several circuits in cross-canter or on the wrong lead, which can lead him to slide and fall.

Alternatively, it is possible to set up a work space inside a larger arena, using jump standards and poles or plastic tape. All **doors and gates need to be closed** and **no other horses** should be present at the same time.

Even when using the highest level of safety precautions, it is always possible that the horse may try to get away from the trainer. Considering the speed and strength of a horse's reactions, the trainer may need to let go of the long reins. If other horses are in the arena, this could create dangerous situations.

How to Proceed

In order to avoid difficult situations, it is important to act with a lot of foresight when attaching long reins for the first time.

Instructing the Assistant

Important!
The safety of all participants is the number one priority.

Until long-reining is consistently possible in a safe and controlled manner, an assistant needs to be present. The most important task of this assistant is to hold the horse while the long reins are attached, and to calm and praise the horse. The plan needs to be discussed and agreed upon in advance to avoid dangerous situations and allow everyone to react optimally.

Situations may arise when long-reining young horses that would be difficult for a trainer to handle alone. The horse may jump over a line or suddenly turn around and wrap himself up. It's necessary to stay calm and have the assistant hold the horse while repositioning the long reins.

Here, the assistant holds the horse while the trainer attaches the long reins.

Leg Protection

As a rule, all four legs need to be protected. To protect the front legs, boots or bandages can be used.

If a horse wears shoes in the back, his legs need to be wrapped using quilts under the bandages. Otherwise, the horse can injure himself when kicking out. When using boots, the long reins can get caught on the buckles of the boots, and the effectiveness of the outside long rein in particular will be impeded.

Familiarization in Three Steps

Longeing surcingles with rings only set high on the surcingle are completely inappropriate for introducing young horses to long-reining.

Step One

- Since most horses go better to the left, start with that direction.
- In order to create steady guidance on the circle, start by attaching the inside long rein from the bit ring to the surcingle. This setup guides the horse along the line of the circle, similar to a single longe line.

Important!
When first introducing the horse to long reins, under no circumstances should a long rein be set up around the hindquarters; horses react unpredictably to this when it is unfamiliar, no matter their usual temperament.

- When working on a circle, the outside long rein is laid over the saddle or surcingle, and then runs from the girth carabiner or surcingle to the bit ring. The long reins have to be set low to keep the outside rein from sliding up under the tail or over the croup onto the horse's back should the horse kick out or buck.

It is best to proceed in three steps when attaching long reins for the first time. I will explain how to do it on a circle first, in a "double-longeing" setup.

The setup for the inside long rein in step one. This longeing circle work area was built using simple jumps.

The setup for the outside long rein—for now, it runs over the saddle.

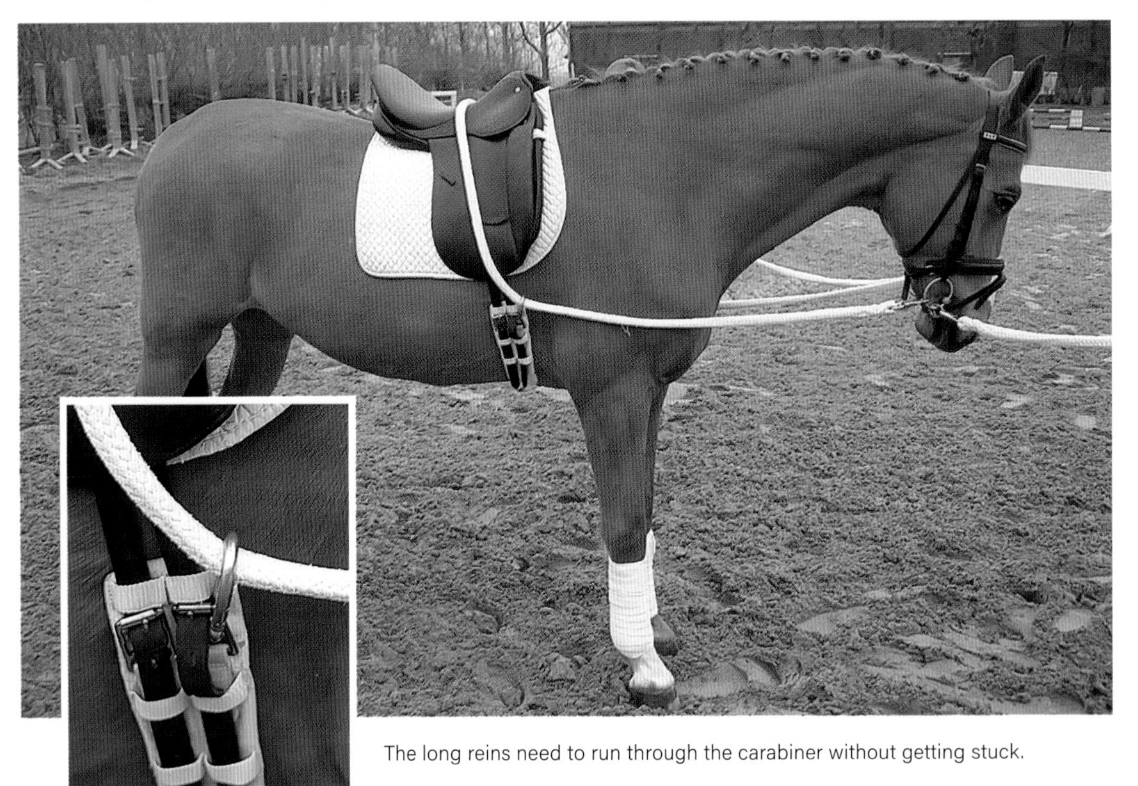

The long reins need to run through the carabiner without getting stuck.

Attaching a rein to the inside and outside of the bit allows for relative control, although an excess of forward energy, exuberance in movement, and occasionally some tension will show up. The inside long rein keeps the horse securely on the line of the circle.

Step Two

Once the trainer feels she can safely control the horse, the outside long rein can be carefully placed around the hind end. There is no one correct time to do this; many horses tolerate it after just a few minutes, but others need a lot more time.

- To get the horse accustomed to the touch of long reins around the hind end, the horse needs to be standing still.
- The assistant should hold and calm the horse while the trainer carefully places the outside long rein on the back of the horse, close to the croup, and pets the hind end. While petting the haunches, the trainer should closely observe the horse's reactions to assess possible objections.
- When placing the outside long rein, the trainer needs to expect a lightning-fast reaction from the horse, and has to be prepared to let the long rein run to the end.
- The outside long rein that is going to cause any reaction that occurs needs to be held very loosely.

Horses react very differently. Many horses accept long reins without any problems. However, the trainer always has to be prepared for energetic, forward movement due to the unfamiliar touch of the long rein. Should the outside long rein slide under the tail and get stuck there, only loosening the long rein immediately will allow the horse to let go of it.

Some horses will have a tendency to rush. During this phase, the trainer only has a little influence in this situation. The horse needs to be calmed down with voice commands, and must find a calm rhythm by himself.

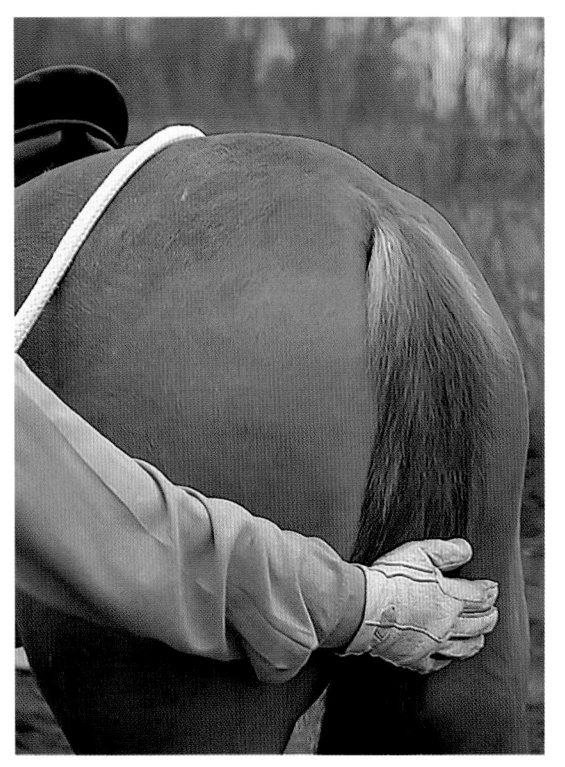

While petting the hindquarters, the trainer leaves the long rein placed on the croup.

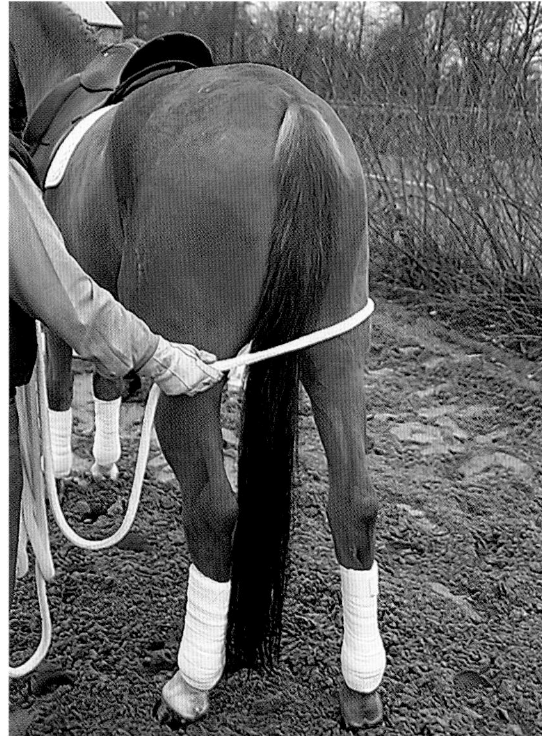

The long rein is carefully placed around the haunches.

This horse shows an immediate reaction when first touched by a long rein around his haunches.

It would be wrong to use forceful aids to control the horse. All the trainer should do is gently give and take—mostly on the inside long rein—to regulate the tempo, while the outside long rein should only be shortened with great care; at this point, since it is touching the haunches, it will only push the horse forward more.

Typical reactions when a horse is first worked on long reins on a circle.

After the initial reaction of kicking out, some horses will react by shortening their steps and slowing down. In this situation, the trainer needs to be very careful with the outside long rein, and must allow the horse time to get used to this new situation.

Step Three

Once the trainer feels she is in control of the horse, the setup for the long reins changes.

- The inside long rein will move to mirror the outside long rein, running from the surcingle to the bit ring.
- It is a good idea to let an anxious horse stand still while he is praised by the assistant. The horse will relax and start to trust that the reins will not hurt him.
- Afterward, the horse should be long-reined on a circle ("double-longed") for a few minutes to give him the opportunity to get used to this new type of work and the setup of the long reins. How long to continue with this procedure depends on the behavior of the individual horse. In any case, the trainer needs to be sure she can control the horse.

- Once the horse has gotten used to the new setup of the long reins and is calm enough to come down into a walk, try a change of direction.

- For these first attempts, it is advisable to use a shorter whip. It is easier to handle, and the horse will not be unnecessarily frightened. The trainer will need to have a whip at hand even when long-reining a horse for the first time, since there is no way of knowing if or how the forward-driving aid will be necessary ahead of time. For this purpose, place the whip on the ground in the center of the longeing area in advance. Of course, you need to be very careful when picking up the whip; stay well outside the reach of the horse's hind legs. It is safest to let your assistant hand you the whip. It can also be helpful to have the assistant handle the whip, if a horse is still coming off the circle or is lacking in forward energy.

Problems seldom arise when horses are taken through a change of direction for the first time, but the trainer needs to be very secure with handling long reins.

After 20 minutes, the horse is already quite relaxed; he could reach forward and down even more than he currently is. All in all, this is a very positive result for this horse's first time working on long reins.

Once the horse is easy to keep on the circle, it is possible to switch to one-handed rein handling.

In my experience, the horse's tensions disperse after a few rounds of long-reining on a circle. The voice should be used to calm the horse and encourage trust.

- Once the horse is mostly relaxed and moves steadily on the circle, a one-handed hold for the long reins becomes possible.
- If, after approximately 20 minutes, the horse has gotten used to this new exercise and shows the first signs of relaxation, it is time to end his first session.
- By praising and rewarding the horse, you can deepen his trust in this work. In some cases, it may be necessary to work with very sensitive horses for a few days without placing the outside long rein around the haunches.

During the first few "double-longeing" sessions, you may observe the horse positioning his head to the outside. This is not of any concern at this point.

This outside positioning of his head allows the horse to stay balanced if his tempo is fast.

The goal is to create secure positioning to the inside and lateral bend on the circle, which will allow the horse to stay balanced and encourage his inside hind foot to reach forward farther, underneath the horse's center of gravity. This is only possible when the trainer is able to apply forward pushing aids and use the whip toward the shoulder as an outward moving aid.

As a rule, long-reining is done with a whip. The whip should be long enough to allow the trainer to touch the horse anywhere on his body, with any intensity she chooses, without effort. Once the ground rules are established, it is best to use a telescope whip 7 to 8 meters (20 to 25 feet) long (see p. 28). This kind of whip is lightweight and easy to handle with precision. The correct movement of the horse and his success in cooperating with the trainer's requests depend on the activity of his haunches. Therefore, the whip is always part of long-reining.

Using a whip correctly is an art that requires years of practice. The trainer needs to know the reflex points of her horse and be able to use the whip in a way that takes the sensitivity of the horse into account. Success doesn't come with forceful forward driving aids, but rather with the ability to touch the horse in a specific place so that he can accept the aid.

Important!
If you are not practiced in handling long reins, let a skilled trainer work with young horses or horses that are new to long-reining.

To introduce horses to work with long reins, the trainer must be skilled and experienced with handling the long reins, and able to manage the horse's reactions with sensitivity and calmness.

Depending on the level of the horse's training, his education will continue individually. If you are working with a young horse that is still in the familiarization phase, the goal is to reinforce his basic training in walk, trot, and canter. It would be wrong to immediately move on to difficult exercises. When you are working with an older horse that has had a correct basic education, it is possible to move to more advanced work quite quickly.

7 Advanced Work with Long Reins

Requirements

The use of long reins has been very successful in advanced work. After basic training is complete—that is, once the horse has learned to rhythmically move in the walk, trot, and canter without tension and with natural self-carriage—this phase of the horse's education can begin.

A four- **or five-year-old horse** should, if started correctly, fulfill these requirements.

Skilled long-reining can make work under the saddle or in front of a carriage much easier. This **horse-friendly** work can improve **suppleness** tremendously. The horse can learn exercises that will be easier for him to execute without the weight of a rider.

At this point, it needs to be said again that long-reining is never done for its own sake. The goal is harmonious collaboration between horse and human, which will encourage better performance by the horse in both competition and recreational riding.

Looking at the training scale, the first three elements have already been achieved, and we are now moving on to:

- Impulsion
- Straightness
- Collection

The horse shows clear signs of tension, and needs to be warmed up further before moving into the working phase of the training session.

The horse shows the main signs of relaxation and suppleness. Advanced work can begin.

Warm-Up Phase

Principally, the warm-up phase precedes all work. It needs to be adapted to each horse individually. Age, level of training, conformation, and temperament all play a role. Below, I will give a general example of a possible warm-up phase:

- Similar to a ridden warm-up, the horse must walk in both directions until he is moving easily.
- As a rule, trot work will follow. The advantage of using long reins on the circle ("double-longeing"), compared to regular longeing methods, lies in the trainer's ability to let the horse stretch by giving with the reins.
- Once the horse moves steadily and with control in the trot, it is time to develop trot-to-canter and canter-to-trot transitions.
- A change of direction should be done every few minutes. The ability to ask for a smooth change of direction is a specific advantage of long reins, and this maneuver can be executed in the walk and trot. This improves the horse's suppleness and creates an additional opportunity for gymnastic exercise.

During a change of direction, especially in the trot, it is imperative for the trainer to be able to focus exclusively on assessing the horse's way of going; the handling of the long reins and the whip has to happen automatically.

Use of additional reins or attachments is not recommended, since the goal is to see and feel correct contact and reactions in the horse. The contact should be so light that the trainer only feels the weight of the long reins in her hands. In much the same way as the inside rein when riding, the inside long rein, in collaboration with the forward pushing aid of the whip, controls the horse's positioning to the inside. The outside long rein has a guarding function—it wraps around the haunches, and therefore supports lateral bend.

Once the horse moves rhythmically and relaxed in the walk, trot and canter, drops his neck and swings through the back, the working phase can begin.

Working Phase

The objective of the working phase of a training session is to improve acceptance of all aids. First, the elements of impulsion and straightness need to be improved in order to guide the horse toward secure lightness and toward collection.

Important!
The following work will only be successful once the typical signs of relaxation and suppleness are observed in the horse.

The value of long-reining work on the circle lies in the opportunity to change direction often, and to work the horse symmetrically in both directions, among others. This encourages the straightness of the horse on the line of the circle. Whichever direction poses more difficulties for the horse should be worked slightly more often than the direction he finds easier. The horse tracks up with his hind end toward the forehand. The outside long rein, by working as a guard, improves his lateral bend and the bend in his ribs.

A working phase could look like this:

Transitions

First, transitions between the basic gaits of walk, trot, and canter will be refined.

Then, tempo changes within the gaits are practiced. A special focus is placed on the evenness of the horse's trot steps. Extension should only take half of the circle; when asking the horse to shorten, the focus needs to be on his self-carriage. The trainer needs to immediately give after shortening the long rein, get light, and push forward.

In the canter, extension can take a whole circle. The canter stride should widen, and the horse needs to be allowed to lengthen his frame.

By practicing transitions, the trainer can improve the activity of the haunches—that is, the increased swinging of the haunches—and the activity of the back. The horse will move with more impulsion.

Halts

Start by practicing full halts from the walk. The horse should stand straight, pointed forward. Since the horse is moving on a circle, the long reins need to be handled in a way that allows him to do so. To practice this exercise, the horse is asked to halt at a specific point in the arena repeatedly. These halts need to be prepared for with several half-halts, as in riding. The horse should learn to react to aids as if they were road signs. A horse that is prepared in this way will also accept the aids for a full halt from the trot.

A secure full halt.

The horse will accept the aids more easily if transitions from trot to halt are again practiced in the same spot in the arena.

If a rider is challenged to transition to a full halt, it is easy to imagine that it will go more smoothly following these exercises. The voice plays a large role. Horses listen more to tone of voice than to any specific word, although they will remember individual words like "halt."

Preparation for a Simple Change of Lead

The transitions from walk to canter and canter to walk are easy to practice in preparation for a simple lead change.

First, the horse is asked several times to transition to canter from trot, in the same spot. Then, a transition to the walk is built in ahead of that specific spot. Generally, the horse will now pick up the canter from the walk at that spot, with the aids given by the trainer.

The canter depart should be uphill, and the transition back to walk should be without extra steps in between. In order to be successful at this exercise, the horse must already be capable of a certain level of collection in the canter. It is appropriate here to long-rein on a smaller circle, since this will make the inside hind pick up more weight on the circle, and therefore the horse will develop greater self-carriage.

Vocal Aids

Even though you shouldn't ride using verbal aids, in order to encourage the horse to react to seat, leg, and rein aids, it can be very helpful during the training phase to use the voice quietly—as if longeing—as an additional support.

Since horses are flight animals, they have very sensitive hearing, and can hear sounds that are barely detectable for humans. This means the voice can be used very quietly. As long as the same acoustic signals are used when riding as on the long reins—for example, a double kiss for the canter depart—the horse will pick up the canter more readily under the rider.

Toward the end of the warm-up phase, the horse is getting a little short in the neck, and is coming onto his forehand.

Height of Attachment—Mechanical "Rollers"

When the long reins are attached at normal height, some horses have the tendency to get too low and short in the neck, and to come onto the forehand after the warm-up phase or after working for some time. In these cases, it is necessary to restore the horse's self-carriage. Using long reins with "mechanical rollers" to attach to the surcingle, as shown on p. 30, is recommended. This system allows for higher attachment of the long reins, adapted to the individual horse (see pp. 31-32). The "rollers" allow for smooth redirection. As already mentioned, frictional resistance at the attachment rings on the surcingle is dramatically reduced. If the long reins are used without these mechanical rollers, this frictional resistance would lead to the horse getting short in the neck.

Frictional resistance and the weight of the long reins have a relatively big impact on the contact with long reins. Horses with an underdeveloped neck and a tendency to get too short should be long-reined with lightweight long reins with mechanical rollers on the surcingle. Otherwise, the high level of frictional resistance means the trainer giving with the long reins reaches the horse's mouth with a time delay, or not at all. This leads to the horse getting too short in the neck, and going onto his forehand. This issue needs to be recognized quickly and mitigated.

During collection, it is important to set the horse's poll in an elevated position. The horse should move with relative elevation. Mechancial rollers are also used to reach this goal. Attaching them higher on the surcingle allows the horse to carry himself higher. The forward-driving aids need to be used sparingly but decisively to ensure relative elevation.

The Trainer Shapes the Horse

This phase requires more effort from the horse, and should not be extended for too long. Just as when working under saddle, the horse has to gradually develop the musculature and physical strength to do this type of work. Horses who start out with strong musculature on the lower neck and poor musculature in general will develop extremely positively with consistent and correct work on long reins. Thanks to improved participation of the back musculature, horses with a tendency to rush will also move with more elasticity, and their movements will become calmer, bigger, and more expressive.

Important!
The horse cannot be allowed to move with extreme elevation, a braced back, and tight musculature of the lower neck.

Addressing Problems in the Walk

Once the long reins are attached in a high position in the trot and canter—for example, to work on collection—this may lead to tension and loss of rhythm in the walk.

Since the walk is particularly sensitive to any disturbances, a relaxed, rhythmical stride is paramount. If a horse braces his back when the long reins are positioned higher, there is a danger of losing rhythm in the walk, or even pacing. This can be addressed immediately by setting the long reins lower on the surcingle, which allows the horse the necessary space to stretch. Generally, this lower setting is preferred, as it results in a ground-covering, relaxed walk.

Tense, incorrect walk. This needs to be addressed immediately by setting the long reins lower.

Test Under Saddle

Important!
The best way to test the success of work on the long reins is to ride or drive the horse immediately following the long-reining session.

Riding or driving immediately following long-reining allows you to determine whether reactions and behaviors observed on the ground can be reproduced by the rider or in front of the carriage. As a rule, the feeling should be much improved with this preparation, and the exercises the horse has already practiced on the long reins will turn out well without much effort. If improvement is not shown, it is worth asking whether the necessary systematic approach was applied.

Don't expect a miracle when working with long reins. This work is simply a valuable support when training horses. In the end, the rider educates the horse.

If you want to progress, it is important to consistently evaluate your own skill as a rider. Successful sessions on long reins are no substitute for light, coordinated aids from the rider!

Time is also a factor in the horse's success. Often, the patience of the trainer, as well as her competence with different training methods, will be tested. If one method of training has been identified as working well for the horse, it is important to stick with it. Experience will show that patience is rewarded with success.

Cool-Down Phase

If the horse will not be ridden after working on the long reins, you proceed to the cool-down phase. Now it is important to allow the horse to stretch long and low, to ensure total relaxation and end on a positive note; this will create the best conditions for the next session.

Introductory Exercises for Long-Reining

Once the elements of rhythm, suppleness, and contact are established, it is time to start with some preparatory exercises for long-reining. The goal of working on long reins from the ground is improved impulsion, straightness, and development of collection. Acceptance of the aids and lightness will improve likewise.

Work on the long reins, following a warm-up on the circle.

Transition from Work on the Circle

- Before moving from work on the circle to work throughout the arena, the horse is warmed up.
- Then the long reins are gathered in medium-sized loops to prevent the horse or trainer from stepping in them and getting caught.
- I recommend using a groundwork whip, rather than a longeing whip, for long-reining throughout the arena. A groundwork whip approximately 2.2 meters (7¼ feet) long, of the type often used in driving, is recommended.
- It is a good idea to show the horse the whip while he is standing still, and carefully touch him with the whip. This creates trust, and the trainer can get a clear impression of the horse's sensitivity.
- When not working on a circle, the trainer walks behind the horse, at a safe distance of approximately 2 meters (6 feet).

The trainer walks behind the horse, at a safe distance of approximately 2 meters (6 feet). The horse is accepting the aids.

Appropriate long rein and whip management.

An assistant helps keep the horse on the rail and get him used to this kind of work.

- Start by having an assistant lead the horse on the rail. Since the trainer is in the horse's blind spot, some tension can arise. It is best to react calmly and thoughtfully to quickly resolve any confusion.
- First walk-to-halt transitions should be practiced. When standing, the horse is praised by the assistant. If possible, the horse should be halted correctly.
- The next phase can include short trot sequences—just a few steps.

Exercises That Put the Horse on the Aids

Once the horse is familiar with this work, he will readily stay on the rail without the assistant. All exercises will now be repeated without an assistant.

The horse moves through the corner with correct positioning and bend.

Leaving the rail for a volte (small circle) with exemplary lateral bend.

Good control of the horse is an important prerequisite for long-reining. It should not be difficult to demonstrate basic arena movements, correct corners, voltes (small circles of 6, 8, or 10 meters in diameter), or half-circles to change direction.

Again and again, you will see horses move away from the rail when working in one direction. This is a sign of tension, which can have a variety of causes. Sometimes, a lack of energy in the trainer's walking pace hinders the horse's natural forward tendency. The newness of this activity and the horse's uncertainty about it may also make him tense; in this case, it will subside by itself. Having the assistant lead the horse and a thorough warm-up phase on the circle can both be helpful in this situation. Just as when working on the circle, success when long-reining in other areas of the arena depends on the correct coordination of the aids. As you progress, the aids will become more and more finely attuned.

Reflex Points

It is important to be familiar with each horse's reactions to the groundwork whip. Horses can show a variety of responses.

In the upper area of the horse's body—**from the hocks up**—the whip has a **forward-pushing effect.** Used in the **lower area,** the whip encourages more energy from the haunches. When used on the sides of the horse, the whip has a forward-sideways, fully sideways, or guarding effect.

Typical reflex points, which cause the horse to lift his hind legs and step farther underneath himself and toward his center of gravity are:

- **at the fetlock**
- **at the hind cannon bone, underneath the hock joint** (superficial flexor tendon)
- **above the hock** (hamstrings)
- **on the croup**—touching here can lead to the horse stepping farther underneath himself, but also can lead to a bounce upward.

As a keen observer on the ground, you can see many reactions that may also be useful when riding.

Reflex points (as seen in *Longieren, Richtlinien für Reiten und Fahren* [Longeing, Guidelines for Riding and Driving], volume 6, page 175).

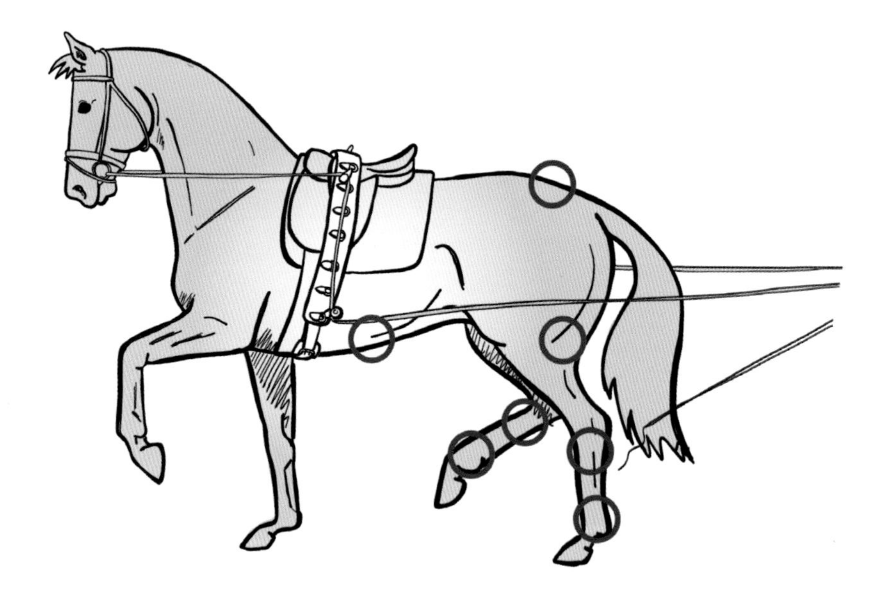

Leg-Yield

To improve acceptance of the forward-sideways moving aids, **leg-yields** can be practiced on long reins.

The forward-sideways movement and "guarding" functions of the rider's leg are performed by the whip.

When asking the horse to yield to the aids on the left side, the request for forward-sideways movement is made by the whip on the left side, and the whip is used for guarding on the right side of the horse.

The whip and the long rein aids have to work together to result in the horse moving at an angle of 45 degrees, forward and sideways.

Willing leg-yield to the left. The trainer is positioned behind the horse in a way that allows the whip to touch either side of the horse as necessary.

In order to improve the angle along the rail in the right leg-yield, the horse is touched on the right side, the moment the right hind leaves the ground. This encourages a forward-sideways movement. During the first try here, you can see the horse twisting slightly in the poll and getting too short in the neck.

To introduce this exercise, the horse can be led out of the corner and set up at the angle needed for the leg-yield.

If a rider struggles to get the horse to accept the forward-sideways movement aids, this is a very appropriate exercise that will improve the horse's reaction to the leg aid asking for sideways movement.

Change of Direction

The change of direction is best done by long-reining a **half-circle to reverse** or, depending on the level of training of the horse, a **large turn-on-the-haunches**.

The turn-on-the-haunches requires a solid relationship between trainer and horse, based on trust. It is relatively easy to develop by gradually decreasing the size of a half-circle in reverse—the difference is that positioning and bend in the direction of travel must be maintained throughout the exercise. Here, special attention must be paid to active engagement of the hind end and a steady rhythm.

Shoulder-In

As soon as the leg-yield is well established, the shoulder-in can be introduced. In shoulder-in, the horse moves forward and sideways along the rail, with the lateral bend of a volte. The trainer can clearly observe the correct angle by walking behind the horse. The outside front leg and inside hind leg should move on the same track.

Shoulder-in is especially valuable in the advanced training of the horse and rider. It improves:

- Relaxation
- Shoulder movement
- Self-carriage
- Straightness
- Collection
- Acceptance of all aids

An exemplary demonstration of shoulder-in with correct positioning and bend. The inside hind and outside front are visibly moving on the same track.

Shoulder-in is a core exercise for advanced riding, and a prerequisite for advanced lateral movements such as travers (haunches-in), renvers (haunches-out), and half-pass.

These exercises create understanding and trust in the horse for the interplay of the forward moving aids and the guarding aids. Thus, the requirements are in place to develop "half-steps" all the way to piaffe and passage.

Important!
Success will require progressing in small, systematic steps, keeping the horse's level of training in mind.

Other lateral movements can be developed on long reins, but they require a much higher level of training from the horse.

8 Training the Driving Horse on Long Reins

Today, horses have lost their relevance as carriage horses, to transport goods, or to work in agriculture, except in rare cases. When speaking of driving horses nowadays, we are mostly talking about sport horses. The driving horse has to be trained to meet the requirements of the FEI internationally.

Important!
The training goal for a driving horse is a high-performing and cooperative horse. The horse should be able to compete for many years, with a foundation of systematic and sensible training.

Here, the foundation to guide the education of driver and horse is laid. There is a special focus on the Training Scale, which we discussed in detail in chapter two (p. 5)—it has equal importance for the driving horse.

Franz Honecker, multi-driving champion of Rheinland and Nordrhein-Westfalen, with the horses Fresco and Eddy.

The six elements of the Training Scale need to be established, both over the entire lifetime of training and within each unit of training.

Safety

All driving horses, not just competition horses, need to be trained following these criteria. When choosing a driving horse, particularly for pleasure, temperament and character are especially important. If a horse bucks or bolts when in harness, the consequences can be dire. That is why the training of the driving horse needs to be undertaken with much care. Safety always comes first.

Importance of the Training Scale for Driving Horses

Rhythm

A forward, ground-covering walk with four clear beats is desirable in a driving horse, whether on the bit or on loose reins.

The **trot** should be rhythmical, with impulsion and elasticity. In a dressage test, working trot, collected trot, and extended trot are all required.

The canter is not required in tests and is therefore not that important. But if a horse is well trained and reliably listens to the driver's aids, the canter can be advantageous when competing on an obstacle course or a cross-country course.

Suppleness

Only a relaxed horse will engage and relax his musculature correctly and cooperate fully.

Contact

A relaxed horse lowers the neck, particularly in the walk, and creates a soft, elastic connection to the driver's hand. A long and low position is desired, as this allows the horse to take big strides.

In the working trot, the horse should show himself in natural self-carriage, when collected he should show relative elevation, and during extended trot, his frame should lengthen.

You can often see driving horses that are much too short in the neck. This hinders a freely forward-swinging hind leg. It's often due to harsh bits and incorrect use of curb chains on curb bits.

Impulsion

Impulsion is the energetic impulse that comes from the hind end and through a swinging back to contribute to the overall forward movement of the horse.

Just as for the riding horse, the importance of a swinging back cannot be underestimated for the driving horse. Observing the back will make it very clear whether a horse is correctly trained, with a back that can swing freely. The horse also needs to accept the aids willingly in all transitions.

Under no circumstances should a driving horse be driven in a forced way during the extended trot; this will result in loss of rhythm, and the horse will end up bracing against the lines, swinging his hind legs out, and stepping wide.

Straightness

The driving horse should also adjust to all straight and bending lines from his poll to his tail, and allow for positioning and bend in both directions. This supports safety, enables symmetrical exercise of both sides, and is a prerequisite for collection.

However, unlike the rider, the driver doesn't have the same direct aids with which to influence the horse's straightness. You will often see driving horses flex or bend correctly in only one direction. Frequently one sees a horse bent to the outside.

Straightness can be greatly improved through switching positions, correct dressage driving, riding, and, especially, working on long reins.

Precision gives the driver the ability to react quickly and safely in all areas of driving.

Collection

The collected tempo in the trot is often driven slowly and shallowly. Very seldom can you observe a genuinely shortened trot with impulsion and relative elevation.

Of course, we need to take the circumstances into account; a horse cannot be expected to show cadence, lightness, and expressive movement while pulling a carriage uphill or in deep footing.

Preparation on Long Reins for Driving and Hitching

Long reins are not absolutely necessary in the education of the riding horse, although they have many benefits. Long reins are, however, a must in the education of the driving horse. They are used the same way as on all young horses, to familiarize the young driving horse with all pieces of equipment during the introduction and trust-building phase.

Where this phase is followed with the first work under saddle for the riding horse, the driving horse is being prepared for hitching. Long reins are the only tool that allows the horse to be safely familiarized with lines and straps.

First Long-Reining with a Bridle

Initially, the horse will be long-reined with an open bridle so he can see the whip, get used to it, learn to respect it, and understand how the different aids work together. Later, a bridle with blinkers can be used.

Working Through the Training Scale

A high level of dressage training is of immense benefit for the driving horse. But the driver's only aids are voice, whip, and lines (reins). In this respect, long-reining offers the ideal conditions to supplement driving training. Long reins allow for targeted development and improvement of each element on the Training Scale. Acceptance of the aids and suppleness in particular can be optimized, and the driver's control over the horse can be improved. A horse with correct training will offer the highest level of precision and safety, and will therefore be more successful, whether he is competing in driving dressage, driving an obstacle course in the arena, or driving cross-country.

The following exercises are of particular importance for the driving horse, and can be developed and improved on long reins:

Transitions—Tempo and Transitions Between the Gaits

The focus should be on walk-to-trot transitions, as well as lengthening and shortening in short sequences (approximately half a circle).

Working trot with impulsion and secure self-carriage.

Prompt Reaction to the Aids

Voice, whip, and long rein aids need to work together with less and less effort. First and foremost, signals in driving are provided by the voice, using specific words and tones of voice.

Safety with a Light Contact—Improving the Horse's Carriage

A driving horse should never be tight in the contact. Contact can be improved through activation of the haunches, and by giving with the long reins.

Incorrect contact can be improved by adjustment of the height at which the long reins attach to the surcingle.

Improvement of Positioning and Bend

Here, it is possible to address the tendency of many driving horses to go with a counter-bend. The whip at the shoulder influences the horse to move out, while the inside long rein provides the necessary positioning to the inside. The outside long rein prevents the hindquarters from falling out, which improves lateral bend.

Change of Direction Through the Circle in Collected Trot

This exercise improves suppleness and the ability to react quickly. It also provides great training for the driver, since she needs to be able to change direction while focusing exclusively on the horse. Management of the reins and whip needs to happen automatically.

A Safe, Square Halt and Standing Still

This is an absolute must for all driving horses—for example, when halted to salute during a dressage test, or at a traffic light. Horses with a tendency to fidget can be taught to relax by practicing halts and standing still for longer periods of time.

Rein-Back

The rein-back should be demonstrated with straightness, diagonal steps, and willingness. This exercise improves acceptance of the aids, lightness, and collection. Particular attention needs to be paid to backing straight, so the carriage doesn't get crooked. Use of the whip on the outside of the haunches can prevent the hindquarters from falling out.

A calm, secure, square halt.

Accepting, straight rein-back with diagonal steps.

The horse is clearly accepting the inside forward-pushing aids and adjusting laterally to the volte.

Leg-Yield

The driver needs to be able to use the whip—in much the same way the rider would use her lower leg—to move the horse forward and forward-sideways. The trainer lets the horse move forward-sideways down the long side at an angle of barely 45 degrees, with the horse positioned away from the direction of travel. The driver needs to apply these aids repeatedly if a horse tries to evade correct positioning and bend—for example, by spooking.

Voltes and Half-Circles to Reverse

Important!
A well-trained driving horse will allow the trainer to achieve harmony with him and drive with little effort.

Exercises like voltes and half-circles to reverse, which are part of many driving tests, clearly improve positioning, bend, and acceptance of the aids. The whip, much like the lower leg of the rider, encourages sideways movement. The inside long rein provides the correct position by giving and taking, while the outside long rein guards and maintains lateral bend.

Left leg-yield.

Right leg-yield.

The work described here may seem cumbersome at times, but it will have a positive effect on your driving in practice.

9 Long Reins for Vaulting Horses

Correct riding is the best cross-training for the hard work of the vaulting horse. The focus should be on activation of the haunches and an active back.

Important!
As in all successful work with horses, the Training Scale needs to be the basis for the training of the vaulting horse.

Even horses who are not ridden in the usual ways or who are not ridden at all can benefit from long-reining.

Long-reining can be a helpful and effective addition to the training of the vaulting horse.

With long reins, the following points can be improved:

- Rhythm—specifically, the three-beat rhythm of the canter.
- Suppleness—the musculature of the back will greatly improve through work in a long and low frame.
- Contact—the horse's self-carriage can be monitored.
- Impulsion—the energetic participation of the hind end can be improved, especially when cantering for extended periods of time (which is a requirement in vaulting).
- Straightness—specifically, the haunches can be prevented from falling out, while at the same time the horse will develop more strength to carry himself.
- Collection—will be improved by focusing on collecting exercises. A rhythmical and collected canter can be achieved.

Long-reining will also improve and maintain a vaulting horse's health. When working with younger horses, long-reining can be part of preparing the vaulting horse for his future work. If problems occur—for example, with lightness or the canter—they can often be corrected on long reins.

It is especially important:

- to activate the horse's back, which means the height at which the long reins attach to the surcingle is very important;
- to change direction often;
- to work on as large a circle as possible, to avoid too much strain;
- to pay attention to activating the hind end, which is often not possible during vaulting training.

Training of a vaulting group. The horse needs to be of high quality and be very well trained to allow for this level of vaulting.

10 Working Over Raised Ground Poles on Long Reins

Long-reining over raised ground poles can be extremely beneficial. Still, the trainer needs to have a clear set of goals for this work before beginning.

In order to reach those goals, the trainer needs to have an appropriate level of both theoretical knowledge and practical skills. This includes, for example, an understanding of equine biomechanics (so she can correctly set distances between raised ground poles) and knowledge of the effects of changing heights and removing poles from a sequence.

The trainer also needs to be able to correctly assess the horse's physical capabilities in order to work toward correct muscle development. A horse should never be asked for too much. It causes more harm than good.

Prerequisites For the Horse

As a rule, long-reining over raised ground poles should only be attempted with horses who have healthy bones, tendons, and joints. Splint boots, wraps, and possibly bell boots need to be used to protect the horse's legs.

Normally, horses will accept work over raised ground poles without problems as long as they are well prepared. Anxious, resistant, and nervous horses pose a challenge to the trainer's skill when long-reining over raised ground poles.

Work over raised ground poles can be helpful for all horses, whether they are younger or older or working on correcting old mistakes.

Purpose and Value of Working Over Raised Ground Poles

The purpose and value of working over raised ground poles is the **improvement of overall suppleness and relaxation**, and in particular the development of an **active back.** The effect of long-reining over raised ground poles is to stretch the topline.

In order to balance himself, the horse naturally has a tendency to drop his neck. This causes his back to round, and at the same time, his hind legs have to work with more energy to reach over the raised ground poles.

In addition, the following elements will be improved:

Controlled Movement

Even distances between raised ground poles encourage horses with irregular movement to develop rhythm. Slower horses have to use more energy, and fast horses must move with more control.

Muscle Training

The higher steps required for raised ground poles force the horse's musculature to work much harder than on flat ground. Even distances between raised ground poles encourage correct patterns of tension and relaxation of the horse's musculature, too, developing his regularity.

Balance and Surefootedness

The horse will learn to balance himself better on each diagonal pair of legs, encouraged by a higher lift. His motor system is stabilized by his improved balance, and therefore his surefootedness also improves.

Dexterity, Attention, and Agility

As the horse's training progresses, you will observe that he is able to master specific exercises—including raised ground poles—with more and more ease. In much the same way as with cross-country training, young horses can be encouraged to pay more attention and cooperate better.

Reaction and Coordination

Adding raised ground poles changes the requirements of some of the exercises you may already be practicing; the horse learns to adapt and react to new challenges.

Suspension and Cadence

In advanced training, the amount of ground covered during each trot step can be increased by widening the distances between the raised ground poles. Shortening these distances while raising the height of the poles will lead to a longer suspension phase, and therefore improve cadence.

Practical Setup

The following setup has been shown to work well.

A setup to long-rein over one ground pole. The outside boundary prevents the horse from passing the pole to the outside, and the poles on the inside ensure that the horse doesn't evade to the inside.

A setup for four poles: they are placed almost straight, and are fixed in the middles of the blocks to keep them from rolling.

The ends of the poles on the side closer to the center of the circle are placed on the ground, so the long reins will not catch on them. If possible, the horse should trot over the center of the poles.

Long-reining over one pole successfully on the first try.

First Introduction of Ground Poles

As always, the horse needs to be warmed up sufficiently before you begin. When work over raised ground poles is introduced for the first time, have an assistant lead the horse over a single pole on the ground several times.

The assistant will also be needed to help set up and change ground poles and distances, and must be ready to help should problems arise. Note that cavalletti with "x" ends should not be used for this work, since the long reins can catch on the crosses.

Long-Reining Over One Pole

The horse is "double-longed" with long reins over one pole until he trots over it without any tension. Skillful support from the trainer makes this easier for the horse.

When working over raised ground poles, it is particularly important for the trainer to "give" with the long reins, in order to allow the horse the necessary stretch and reach in his neck. The horse uses his neck for balance, and his ability to move his neck should therefore not be hindered.

In order to avoid overwhelming the horse, proceed in small steps. Even if quick success is desired, it cannot be forced. The horse must develop trust in this work and also in the trainer. If he is not at ease, increasingly demanding exercises and ultimate success will not be possible.

The trainer should stick to just one ground pole for the first introductory sessions.

Long-Reining Over Four Poles

Once long-reining over one pole has been mastered, the degree of challenge can be raised by using four poles. Two poles are not an option; horses often simply jump over both, and thus lose their rhythm. If uncertainty and tension arise, the horse should be long-reined next to the poles until he has relaxed again.

The horse is long-reined over four poles for the first time. He is willing, but is not stretching forward and down quite yet.

A positive result for the first session. This outcome should be satisfying, and the session can end with lots of praise for the horse.

The active lifting of the feet is noticeable.

This height is reserved for horses with enough elasticity.

The distance between the poles, at the center where the horse is stepping, should be about 1.30 meters (4¼ feet) in the trot. This is just a general number; it should be adjusted to suit each individual horse. The recommended height of the poles for this work is 15 to 20 cm (6 to 8 inches). This allows an effortless stepping over for the horse and can be changed according to the length of stride for each horse.

This work needs to be done in both directions equally. The first sessions should be kept short, and the horse should be praised after every successful attempt.

Once the horse has successfully been introduced to working on long reins over raised poles, the foundation has been laid for more refined work.

Work Over Raised Ground Poles as Part of Cross-Training

Work over raised poles is a valuable component of the horse's education. Many riders reject it, because it takes a lot of effort and will not meet success if executed poorly. As a general rule, horses with rushed movement or short strides can improve greatly through continuous work over raised poles. Their movement will become more energetic, and cadence and impulsion will improve. This work should be done regularly, two or three times a week.

In order to guarantee a smooth session, the presence of an assistant is absolutely necessary—for example, to return a pole to the correct position when it shifts, or to help adjust the distances between poles to the individual horse.

Work Over Raised Ground Poles as Part of Advanced Training

During dressage training, the horse's movement can pose a challenge from time to time. If, for example, the challenge lies in creating more collection and cadence in a horse, setting the poles higher—at approximately 25 cm (10 inches)—and shortening the distances between the poles can address this challenge.

This horse's back is swinging optimally over higher poles. The "give" in the long reins allows him to balance perfectly.

Movement with cadence; the horse is still relaxed, and is accepting the aids.

If you are working on improving ground coverage, the poles can be placed farther apart from each other, depending on the horse's potential. Extending and lengthening his steps needs to be practiced in small doses. Otherwise, there is a danger the horse will be overwhelmed, or even injured.

Work over raised ground poles offers variety within the horse's training program, and it is an ideal prerequisite for jumping.

11 Jumping on Long Reins

Along with free jumping and jumping under saddle, jumping on long reins offers an additional opportunity to introduce young horses to jumping and advance experienced horses. It challenges the trainer in similar ways to work over raised poles. The trainer needs to be experienced in working wtih jumping horses, and skillful in managing the long reins and whip. Especially in jumping, it is paramount to progress systematically.

The Relevance of the Training Scale for Jumpers

The Training Scale is applicable for jumpers at every level of training. Following it is a prerequisite for harmonious and successful jumping.

Rhythm Is the Prerequisite for:

- Effective work from the horse.
- Even and rhythmical movement on both straight and curved lines.
- Correct basic tempo throughout the course.

Suppleness Is the Prerequisite for:

- Willingness to perform.
- Correct contact.
- Riding without resistance and tension.
- An active back.
- Correct bascule (curving of the topline during the jump).
- Improvement of reactivity.
- Improvement of coordination.
- Improvement of jumping technique.

Contact Is the Prerequisite for:

- Full acceptance of the aids.
- Lengthening and shortening of the canter stride—for example, to achieve correct distances.
- Neck extension toward the jump.
- Load-bearing capacity, suspension, and speed.

Impulsion Is the Prerequisite for:

- Activity of the back.
- Activity of the haunches.
- Keeping the horse "in front of the aids."
- Secure control at higher speeds.
- Clearance over the jump.

Straightness Is the Prerequisite for:

- Even use of both sides of the body (for maintaining soundness).
- Acceptance of all aids in both directions.
- Riding turns.
- Load-bearing capacity, suspension, speed, and jumping power.

Only after fulfilling these prerequisites can the horse—with straightness, good technique, and bascule—"jump through his body."

Collection Is the Prerequisite for:

- Shifting weight off the forehand (for maintaining soundness).
- Maintaining correct position to the jump.
- Riding tight turns (required during a "jump-off").
- Developing "uphill" jumping power.

The degree to which the horse can improve on long reins depends on his talent. The trainer has to be able to recognize this. Getting overly ambitious when working with a talented horse is dangerous.

Important!
A horse that has been trained following the foundation of the Training Scale offers the highest possible level of precision and safety when jumping a course. This horse will be pleasant to ride, and if competed fairly and conscientiously, will be able to perform for many years.

Here, the old saying **"less is more" applies;** the demands on the horse should increase only on the foundation of a correct education—and only when he is at the appropriate age.

For riders who, for whatever reason, cannot jump their horses themselves, long reins are a fantastic tool to continue training their horses over fences.

Important!
Long-reining effectively over jumps requires both skill and experience from the trainer. The management of the long reins and the whip has to happen automatically.

Jumpers are not the only horses that can benefit from jump training on long reins. This work offers many advantages for horses active in other disciplines—for example, variety in training, and improved relaxation.

Benefits of Gymnastics on Long Reins

Jumping on long reins is a form of gymnastics. When working with inexperienced horses, the focus is on building trust, joy in jumping, safety, and independence. In addition, this work has many benefits for both younger and older horses. For example, it encourages:

- A calm approach to the jump (with a trot pole at approximately a 2.20-meter (7¼-foot) distance).
- Use of the back in the bascule.
- Development and refinement of technique.
- Improved coordination.
- Development of greater focus.
- Improved self-confidence.
- Variety in the horse's training program.

Among other things, horses learn to approach a jump on a curved line in the canter, and to maintain the correct canter lead.

Setup

In order to avoid catching the long reins on obstacles and allow successful jumping, this setup is recommended.

This standard is custom-made—the long reins are able to glide over the rounded part easily.

The cross-rail is inviting, and it helps encourage the horse to jump over the center of the obstacle.

The standards on the outside prevent the horse from evading the jump. This jump can be set up as an upright, oxer, or triple-bar.

First Jumps for the Young Horse on Long Reins

If the horse is familiar with work over raised ground poles, the first exercises in jumping typically don't pose any problems.

Important!
In order to maintain the horse's trust in his training, the difficulty should only be increased very gradually. Overfacing and rushing can lead to serious setbacks. Here, less is more.

The warm-up should take place next to the jump. A height of approximately 30 centimeters (1 foot) is recommended. The cross-rail encourages the horse to jump over the center of the jump.

First, the horse should be led to the jump by the assistant to get familiar with it.

The horse is being warmed up next to the jump. This way, he grows familiar with the obstacle. If a horse gets pushy after the jump, he needs to be long-reined next to it until relaxation and lightness are restored.

Before long-reining the horse over the very first jump, the assistant should lead the horse to the jump and let him stand quietly next to it for a moment.

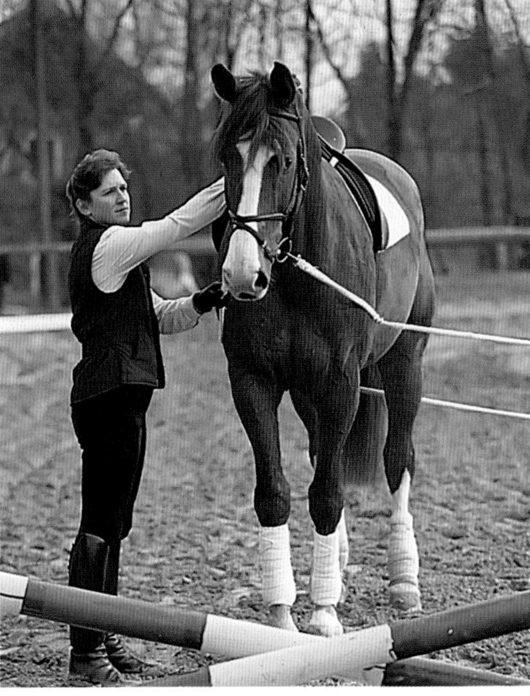

The horse goes over the first jump very willingly. He is jumping too high, but that will improve over time.

Leading him to the obstacle and showing it to him encourages the horse's confidence in jumping.

Then, with skill and patience, the trainer needs to guide the horse to the jump. A lot of "give" is necessary in order to avoid hindering the horse's movement when he jumps. Tension after the first few jumps is completely normal.

If a horse gets pushy or rushes after the jump, he needs to be long-reined next to it until relaxation and lightness are restored. If a horse jumps a small jump without effort, the jump can be raised.

The trainer should be satisfied with a **harmonious final jump.**

Jump series: The trainer demonstrates how to use the long reins to guide a horse with no experience jumping on long reins. This approach allows for immediate success.

Gymnastics: Over this small jump, the horse shows optimal technique. His bascule and leg technique are close to perfect.

Variety in Jump Training

In general, this work is done in both directions, and should start in the direction that is easier for the horse. In order to be successful, follow the principles:

From Easy to Difficult

and

From Familiar to New

If jumping is used to provide variety in the horse's training, or as a warm-up, the height of the jump is not relevant—only harmonious performance of the task matters.

A trot pole in front of the jump incentivizes calm jumping, and improves the technique of the front legs.

During a training session, these elements could, for example, be set up as follows—depending on the horse's talent, the requirements can be made more difficult:

- **Cross-rail** in the trot, height approximately 30 to 40 centimeters (12 to 16 inches), with or without a trot pole; distance to the cross-rail, 2 to 2.2 meters (6½ to 7¼ feet).

- **Small vertical** from the trot, height approximately 60 to 80 centimeters (2 to 2½ feet), with or without a trot pole.

- **Small oxer** from the trot, height approximately 60 centimeters (2 feet).

- Jumping small jumps and oxers from the canter; the trainer needs to pay attention to an even, rhythmical basic tempo.

Jumping from the canter, the horse can "fly" with confidence.

If horses are being schooled for jumping in particular, long reins offer a wide variety of exercises. Building on the foundational exercises, the trainer can improve the horse's technique and bascule. Training sessions can be adapted individually for each horse with different setups.

The technique and reactivity of the front legs can be improved with small jumps from the trot. The power of the horse off the ground can be specifically supported by setting up an oxer; this will also encourage the extension of the horse's body in the air and better technique in the hind legs. An essential benefit of long reins is the opportunity to control the horse before and after the jump. Skillful and generous "give" in the long reins over the jump is required.

Being able to closely observe the horse before, over, and after the jump can provide valuable insight to the rider and trainer. This insight, when correctly acted upon, can lead to clearly improved performance.

Solving Problems

"Strong" Horses

Important!
A rider is seldom able to correct the problems caused by her own riding. As a rule, an experienced jumping trainer should be consulted.

If a horse is "strong" under saddle, and has a tendency to rush to jumps, the warm-up should take place next to the jump. Following the warm-up, the horse should be long-reined over a 50-centimeter (1½-foot) cross-rail. If the horse gets "strong," he should be long-reined next to the jump until he has relaxed again. This can be repeated as necessary. A trot pole can also encourage the horse to jump calmly. Before the jump can be approached at a canter, the horse must be consistently able to make a calm and controlled approach from the trot.

It is surprising how relaxed otherwise "strong" horses can be when they jump without a rider. In this case, the rider needs to look critically at her effect on the horse.

"Soured" Horses

If a horse has lost his enjoyment of jumping under saddle—has gotten "sour," in other words—the following method is recommended:

After the warm-up, the horse should be long-reined over a ground pole. Pay attention and make sure his nose can stretch forward; the horse should not feel held back or hindered. Then, set up a small cross-rail, approximately 30 centimeters (1 foot). From there, how you should proceed depends on the reaction of the horse. Typically, the difficulty can be raised to a small jump soon. If the horse is moving toward the jump and has regained his confidence and interest in jumping, after several training sessions on long reins, he can be jumped under saddle again. You should not ask too much of the horse at first.

12 Corrective Work on Long Reins

There are various reasons why a horse may end up needing corrective work. For example:

1) Faults of conformation:

- A low-set neck with incorrect musculature, problems with bending at the poll, straight haunches, high in the haunches, and so on.

2) Faults in temperament:

- Lack of desire to perform, lack of willingness, strong personality (the horse has trouble listening to the rider), and so on.

3) Rider mistakes:

- Incorrect basic training during the introduction phase (see p. 33).
- Mistakes made during advanced training.
- Insufficient riding skill—for example, the rider cannot maintain the level of training the horse has already reached.

Important!
A rider or driver is seldom able to correct the problems caused by her own riding or driving.

Incorrect application of the aids, even if accidental, often causes problems. In those cases, it is next to impossible to improve the situation if that root cause is not addressed. The best solution is to allow an experienced trainer to point the horse in the right direction. This needs to happen sooner rather than later, since, for example, a tongue problem that has already turned into a habit can be very difficult to correct after enough time has passed.

Important!
With any problem a horse presents, whether it is physical or psychological in nature, it is most important to return the horse to a place of relaxation and cooperation.

In addition, it is important to improve the rider's aids. The best way to do that is with a qualified trainer.

Long reins are very beneficial for horses who need corrective work.

Horses with a strong personality can learn to listen and to pay attention to the requests humans make of them. Stallions naturally want to dominate. Long reins offer a safe way to clarify who is in charge without arguments, and with very little effort.

Important!
Health issues need to be excluded as possible causes before any attempt is made to correct the horse's faults, whatever their nature.

With the necessary skills, many challenges can be reduced or addressed on long reins. Examples include mistakes in a horse's training, faults in temperament, resistance, tension, problems with rhythm and connection, tongue issues, rearing, bucking, and more.

Riding or driving a horse with faults of conformation can be made easier with long-reining.

Correcting existing challenges should always be done by an experienced trainer, under saddle or on long reins.

Especially when correcting existing problems, the trainer needs to be able to recognize the root causes and address them through skillful work on the long reins. Patience and sensitivity, as well as consistency and confidence, are called for.

Before resuming work under saddle or with a carriage, the horse must show signs of relaxation during long-reining. This way, a foundation is laid that can support renewed learning and progress.

No miracles can be expected from long-reining. It would be too easy to assume that long-reining once or twice will result in meaningful success. Depending on the issue at hand, it can take weeks or months to successfully address a problem. Supplemental work on long reins may still be necessary much later.

Example:

I had one very difficult but talented horse that needed six months of problem-solving on long reins. This horse had a strong personality, no desire to perform, and a tendency to evade the aids of the rider by bucking and rearing. To begin with, he had strong musculature on his lower neck and was poorly muscled overall. His trot was short and rushed, and his walk was uneven. All these were typical signs of back problems, especially since the horse had little elasticity and was hard to sit.

At first, the horse was long-reined in a long-and-low frame to address the cause of the problem—his back—and avoid unnecessary risk to the rider. Once the horse showed relaxation and cooperation on the long reins, it was possible to start exercises in preparation for work in hand. At this point in time—10 weeks in—it was already possible to observe an improved topline and increased development of correct musculature. The horse's movement became more supple and ground-covering. Much praise was used while working in hand to reassure the horse that his reactions were correct.

While developing transitions on the long reins (halt, walk/canter, and canter/walk), the horse grew more and more accepting of the aids, and his cooperation increased consistently. After four or five months, the work in hand had improved to a point where, through half-steps, the beginnings of piaffe and passage were recognizable. This clearly helped him develop his musculature. Individual training sessions in hand were kept short, but they happened regularly.

Work in collection was kept light and easy. This allowed for considerable improvement in the physical and psychological prerequisites for continuing training under saddle. The horse, who had initially refused to cooperate and had been deemed "unrideable," was back on track for more training, and turned out to be a pleasant ride.

Going forward, his education under saddle will still be supported by long-reining.

Working with this particular horse made it very clear that with the help of long reins, a gentle correction of horses who present challenges is entirely possible.

Even though it takes tremendous patience and persistence to point horses with difficulties in the right direction, it has been shown time and time again that horses who have a tendency toward resistance during certain training phases turn out to be high performers.

13 Addressing Health Problems on Long Reins

A large number of health issues require the horse to move and work, at the same time that he can't be ridden. In addition, horses who are recovering from injury often need to get back into work without a rider at first. In these situations, long reins offer the opportunity to provide movement and work to the horse in a gradual, controlled, safe way.

The horse needs to be familiar with long-reining. Otherwise, the horse may have a strong reaction to being asked to participate in an unfamiliar activity, which will do more harm than good.

Typical Illnesses

Before starting rehabilitation, any health issues need to be recognized and clearly diagnosed. This requires a veterinarian as part of the team.

Long-reining can be helpful in the case of any one of the following health issues or illnesses:

- Rubs and sores or fungal infections in the saddle area—if possible, use a surcingle rather than a saddle.
- Psychological challenges.
- Restoring fitness during rehabilitation.
- Back problems.

A veterinarian needs to be consulted, especially when you are dealing with an illness that affects the movement apparatus of the horse.

Long-reining offers an effective supplementation to conventional treatment of back problems, and can even be the main means of treatment. With back issues, it is particularly important that the type and cause are investigated and medical treatment is ongoing.

Reasons for Resistance

It is not always easy to diagnose back problems, since pain in that area shows up in many different ways, and is often not recognized as originating in the back.

Many times, horses who are uncooperative due to back pain will be labeled as resistant. The refrain, "He needs to work through this!" is intended to justify the use of sharp bits or draw reins.

Every rider and trainer needs to pay close attention to the mental and physical health of the horse, and do their best to get to the bottom of the issue and address the cause.

The Back as the Center of Movement

The back is the center of movement in the horse. Rhythm, suppleness and relaxation, freedom of movement, softness in the poll, self-carriage, impulsion, elasticity, straightness, collection—all of these depend on an actively swinging back. A healthy back is a requirement for good performance.

If back problems are not recognized in time, they can lead to immense pain and even the retirement of the horse, if irreparable changes to the spine occur.

The Biomechanics of the Back

When we examine the construction of the horse's back, the negative effects of an unrecognized back issue become evident.

The back forms a bridge between the forehand and the haunches. This bridge consists of many vertebrae. Every vertebra has processes of different lengths. They are longest along the withers. The front processes are pointed backward, and the back processes are pointed forward.

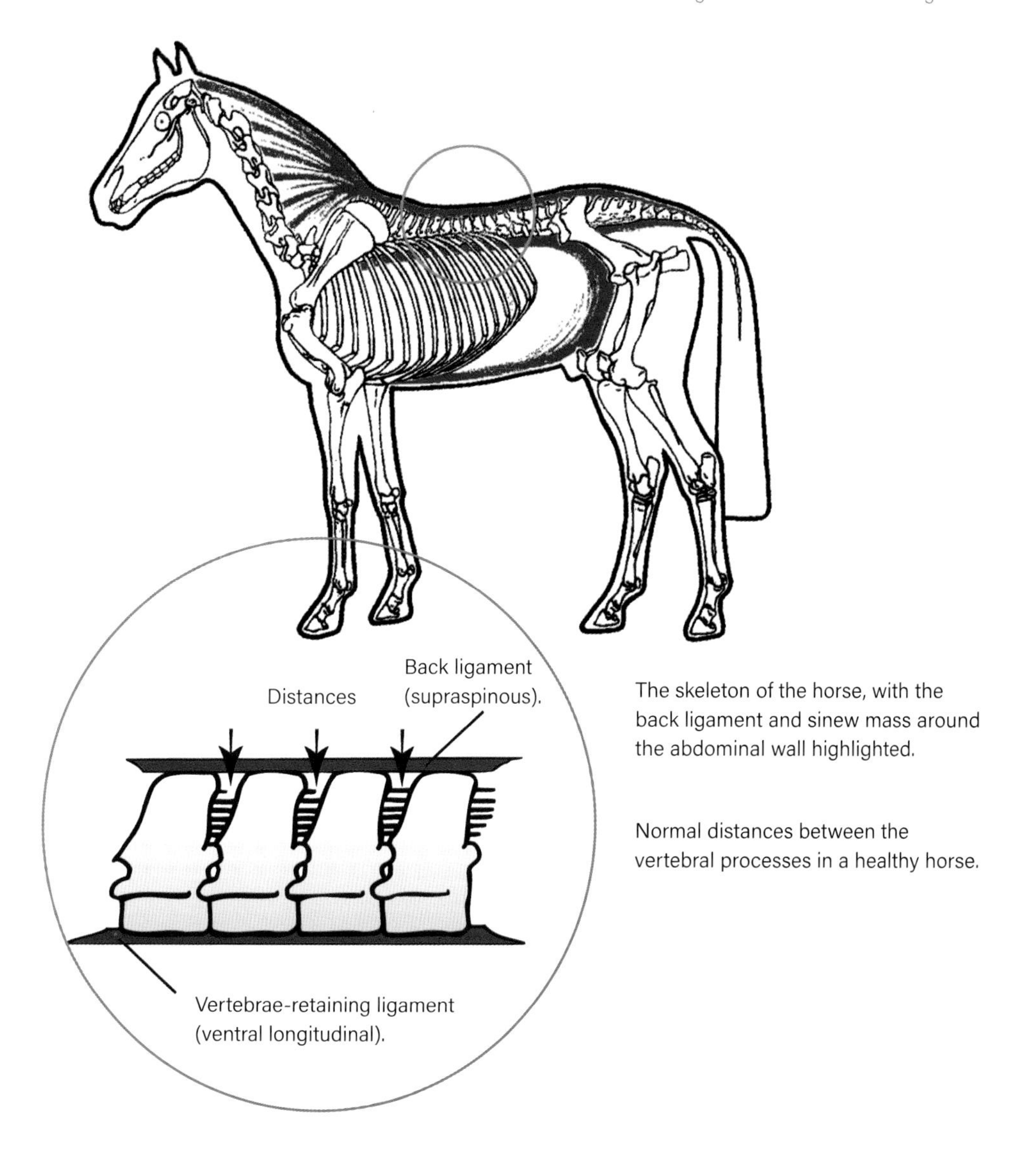

The skeleton of the horse, with the back ligament and sinew mass around the abdominal wall highlighted.

Normal distances between the vertebral processes in a healthy horse.

All vertebrae are connected by the back ligament. Toward the head, the back ligament turns into the nuchal ligament, with its cervical plate.

The supraspinous ligament forms the upper connection of the vertebrae bridge. The ventral longitudinal ligament forms the lower connection of the vertebrae bridge.

Two groups of neck muscles are positioned to either side of the nuchal ligament. They carry the head and neck, and function in the same direction as the nuchal ligament. When the horse stretches the neck forward, the neck musculature and nuchal ligament pull the processes of the withers forward. This pull is transferred to the back ligament, and supported by the transverse spine muscle. All back and lumbar vertebrae have to follow; as a result, the back is raised. The head-neck lever is used for balance, especially when carrying weight. This frees up the musculature of the back and croup to serve their original function: locomotion.

Raising the back is supported by the bottom connection of the vertebrae bridge and the straight abdominal muscle. If the horse, for whatever reason, does not raise his back, the weight of the rider can lead to tension and inflammation of the back musculature, and even sagging of the spine.

Symptoms

Since horses don't have words to tell us if and where they are hurting, the trainer, rider, or driver needs to recognize all signs of deviation from full health in the horse. It is extremely important to catch back problems early on.

Here is a list of 20 symptoms that could point to back problems:

- Sensitivity when groomed and touched.
- Girthiness (biting and kicking).
- Inability to stand still during mounting.
- Dropping or "humping" the back when being ridden.
- Inability to relax.
- Being above the reins, against the rider's hand, or head tossing.
- Discontented, pinned ears.
- Lack of chewing activity when ridden; grinding the teeth; sucking in the tongue.
- Resistance to work; rearing.
- Bolting; bucking.
- Shortness of stride.
- Loss of rhythm.
- Lameness issues.

- Repeated changes of lead into cross-canter.
- Stiffness on one side; difficulty achieving lateral bend.
- Unusual reactivity.
- Sudden blocking of the aids.
- Refusal to accept the aids.
- Unwillingness to collect.

If back problems are present, the cause needs to be investigated.

Causes

The causes of back problems can be found in a variety of areas, and can differ widely in nature. Lameness of all kinds, joint problems, navicular syndrome, hock and stifle issues, dental problems—all of these can lead to the horse going against the rider's hand and bracing his back, which in turn leads to painful tension in the musculature of his back. The same can be caused by poorly fitting tack. The horse's prior training and the ability of the rider or driver also need to be considered.

High expectations too early are a common cause of back problems in younger horses. Horses are fully grown at six years of age. Four- to six-year-olds with a lot of talent are particularly vulnerable. They are often asked to move with a level of collection before they are physically able to appropriately step under with their hind legs. As a result, they may brace their backs, step short in the trot, lose rhythm in the walk, find themselves unable to use their whole bodies in the canter, and develop faulty musculature.

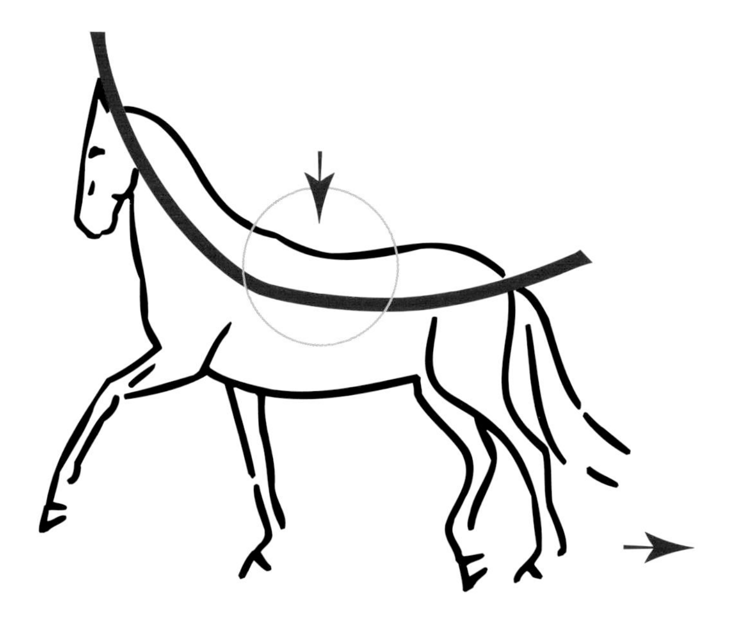

"Kissing spines" can be caused by asking young horses for too advanced a degree of collection, which their musculature is not ready to support, resulting in sagging of the spine.

If, for whatever reason, a horse is ridden in this posture, the back will start sagging downward.

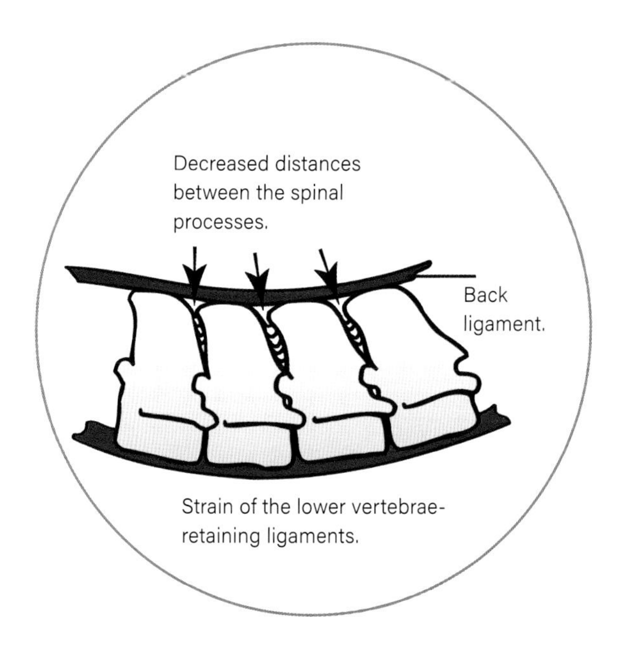

When the spinous processes touch ("kissing spines"), the upper vertebrae and connecting ligaments are compressed, and the lower ones are strained. The friction between the vertebrae is very painful for the horse, and can lead to a limited range of motion in the back.

Effectiveness of Long-Reining

Important!
Correctly executed rehabilitation on long reins can be instrumental in developing the horse's ability to raise his back, and thereby encourages relaxation, stretching, and strengthening of the back musculature.

For rehabilitation and treatment to be successful in the long run, the causes of back problems need to be addressed.

After consulting a veterinarian, long-reining can be helpful in creating a posture in which the horse is able to raise his back (reaching forward and down). This may only be possible without the weight of the rider. Since fixed side-reins are not used when long-reining, the trainer can allow the horse to stretch as much as necessary. By incorporating many changes of direction, one-sided tension can be prevented, and the horse's musculature will develop symmetrically.

In order to prevent back problems, the horse should always be worked in a manner that allows him to raise his back.

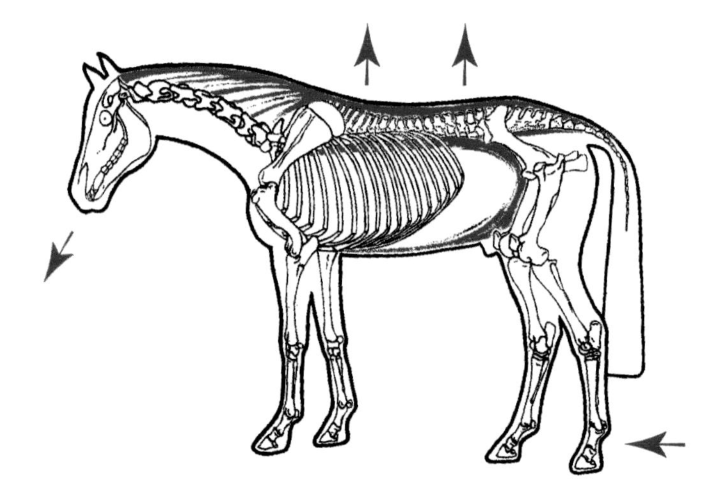

The stretch of the neck forward and down allows the nuchal ligament to straighten the spinous processes, and therefore the back rises—especially if the haunches get activated at the same time.

Activated by the forward driving aids of the rider, the horse moves dynamically and "uphill." The rider should be able to "ride through the back" and on a long rein at all times.

Summary: all young horses, and all horses during the warm-up phase, need to be encouraged to stretch the topline. Pushing, carrying, and suspensory power need to be correctly and slowly developed, without sacrificing a freely swinging back.

14 Development of Piaffe and Passage

The horse should be prepared for this work as described in chapter 7, Advanced Work with the Long Reins (p. 48).

When working on advanced exercises, the transitions between working on the circle and long-reining on straightaways can be fluid. It is quite possible to start the warm-up phase in the "double-longeing" circle scenario and then transition to collected work in other areas of the arena by shortening the long reins.

Important!
It is crucial for the trainer to recognize the horse's limitations when it comes to developing piaffe and passage.

The **talent** and **predisposition** of the horse need to guide the development of piaffe and passage. The trainer needs to proceed systematically and cautiously with each individual horse.

A morning workout on the long reins.

Under no circumstances should this work be done in an attempt to meet some abstract timeline or standard. Not all horses have a talent for piaffe and passage, and they should not be forced into either by applying rough aids.

As for all exercises, the trainer needs to have a clear image of the optimal form and demonstration. The desired ideal of piaffe and passage is described in the "Aufgabenheft Reiten der Deutschen Reiterlichen Vereinigung" [Riding Exercise Book of the German Equestrian Federation]. Point 3.16 in the chapter "Anforderungen an das Reiten in Dressurprüfungen" [Requirements for Riding in Dressage Tests] describes the piaffe as follows:

> **3.16 Piaffe**
> The piaffe is a trot-like movement with elevation on the spot. Increased bend in the haunches is desired. A moment of suspension happens between the moments when each diagonal pair of feet touch the ground.
>
> While the back musculature can swing with elasticity, the hindquarters are lowered and take on increased weight. The poll remains the highest point. The foreleg is raised maximally to a horizontal line, without ever losing the diagonal footfall pattern, and set down vertically. The weight-carrying haunches are energetically raised to the height of the fetlock joints.
>
> The piaffe requires a specific number of steps. A forward tendency needs to be observable. The horse is allowed to step at least one to two hooves forward; some tests allow for the forward movement to be 1 meter (3 feet) in total.

Passage is described as follows:

3.17 Passage
The passage is an elevated trot, with little ground covered and a clear moment of suspension.

In the passage, the horse reaches the highest level of collection and cadence.

Each diagonal pair of legs leaves the ground with spring and energy, and the suspension phase is longer. The foreleg is lifted, as in the piaffe, to a horizontal line, while the lowered hindquarters and closed haunches take on more weight, staying active and energetic.

How to Do It

Since working in collection takes a lot of strength, it should begin right after the warm-up phase. Although the warm-up is important, especially for nervous horses, enough **energy** and **impulsion** has to be saved to allow the horse to work in collection.

A relaxed stride with feather-light contact—one possibility for warming up a horse before work in collection begins.

Warm Up First

The warm-up phase can look different for each horse. Normally, the horse will be worked on the long reins for 15 minutes, until signs of relaxation can be observed.

Very forward horses can also be ridden first. The rider will feel when the horse is accepting the forward-driving aids, and can then begin long-reining.

Some horses do very well with focused, calm work in the walk for a warm-up. The trainer walks behind the horse on the long reins from the outset. By walking behind the horse in a brisk tempo, the trainer encourages the horse to stride and stretch. The horse adjusts to the aids, and is brought into a state of cooperation and focus by practicing accurate arena figures and walk-to-halt transitions.

Careful Beginning

Next, the trainer walks behind the horse at a safe distance (far enough to be out of reach of kicking hooves—approximately 2 meters, or 6 feet). To ensure the horse reacts correctly to the aids and to familiarize the horse with this work, the trainer should practice many **walk-to-halt** and **halt-to-walk** transitions. This also encourages communication between trainer and horse.

The trainer needs to be familiar with the horse's reactions to the whip. The horse should not react with anxiety or panic, and has to trust the trainer enough to accept the whip as an **aid**.

Every horse reacts differently to the touch of the whip, and touching some points may lead to a reflex reaction.

Now, short trot sequences (approximately 5 to 10 steps) can be included. If a horse reacts strongly, he needs to be calmed down by standing quietly, or possibly backing up.

The success of this work depends on the horse moving with correct posture and light contact.

Another view of the reflex points, as described in chapter 7, "Advanced Work with Long Reins" (p. 62).

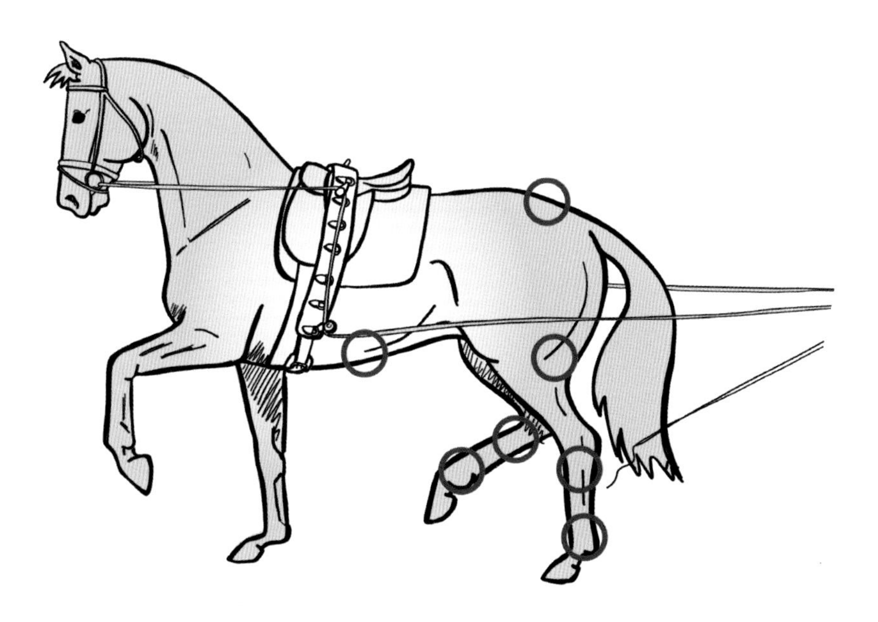

Here is a list of common mistakes or issues in the horse during this phase:

- Too short in the neck.
- Going against the contact.
- Coming onto the forehand.
- Tight, tense contact.
- Getting crooked.
- Leaving the rail.
- Spooking.
- Tension.

In all of these cases, it is important to reinforce the prerequisites by revisiting basic training and shoring up the fundamentals. A longer warm-up phase is often enough. It may be necessary to allow the horse more time to process, or slow down the overall approach. Keep in mind the muscular development of the horse and his intelligence.

This work needs to be adjusted to each individual horse, based on his age, level of training, conformation, suppleness, temperament, nerves, and sensitivity. The success of these efforts is also determined by the skill level of the trainer.

Now, the trot steps will be shortened while their diagonal movement is maintained. Use forward-driving whip and voice aids while shortening the horse's steps with the long reins. It is vitally important to always follow shortening the long reins with "giving" and lightening the contact, in order to ensure the haunches are not blocked from stepping forward. Do not try to encourage the horse by constantly touching him with the whip; this will only result in loss of rhythm and dullness.

Ideally, the horse should continue with the exercise until the trainer deliberately ends it.

Cadenced movement in half-steps.

A good attempt at piaffe. The hindquarters should be lower, and the "uphill" frame can be improved.

A good piaffe, with exemplary bend in the haunches and an excellent frame. The result of systematic training.

The Piaffe

Important!
Success mainly depends on praise and ending the exercise at the right time, again followed by praise.

In the following work, the horse is slowed down—while increasing the bend in the haunches and maintaining energy—until a pause in the cadence can be observed, and forward movement is minimized. Here, it is especially important that the diagonal footfall pattern is maintained. If the horse loses his rhythm, he needs to move forward immediately. **Even a few positive attempts need to be met with praise.**

Depending on his ability, it may be easier for the horse to develop piaffe from a collected walk. In this case, the prerequisites need to be established in the same systematic way.

The number of steps can be increased once the horse has understood the principle behind the movement.

Once the horse has learned to piaffe on long reins, he will soon be able to keep his balance under a rider. This works best if the rider remains passive at first, with an additional helper acting as trainer, using the long reins to give the aids for the piaffe. Gradually, the rider takes over, and the trainer becomes more passive.

The Passage

In order to master passage, a horse needs to bring innate ability to the table, especially a **high level of elasticity**. The passage can be developed from the walk or from a shortened trot with cadence. Pushing power, carrying power, and springiness need to be balanced out by the trainer. This exercise requires skill and experience from the trainer. Passage requires a more pronounced contact than piaffe.

A harmonious overall impression of the horse, with well-developed spring and cadence and optimal suppleness.

The elevation of the foreleg is already very close to perfect.

Lightness and "give" by the hand make dynamic engagement of the haunches and a moment of suspension in the cadence possible.

The horse may get tense in his back and develop stiff steps, a kind of "floating trot." In this case, the warm-up phase needs to be more thorough, and the height at which the long reins attach may need to be lowered—the horse needs to be "rounder." The level of collection can be improved by more encouragement of the hindquarters—for example, through half-steps, or a few steps of rein-back.

Transitions between Piaffe and Passage

Some horses prefer the transition from piaffe to passage, whereas others prefer the transition from passage to piaffe.

The challenge lies in performing both transitions with even steps, without loss of rhythm or impulsion. In order to make this easier for the horse, an attempted passage with little collection should be practiced early on, alternating with shortened half-steps. The horse learns to accept the forward-driving and shortening aids, while maintaining a diagonal footfall pattern during the transitions.

It is important to keep in mind that the development of piaffe and passage are exhausting for the horse. It takes tremendous strength to balance on each diagonal pair of legs while showing cadenced movement. Therefore, this work should not be done over a long stretch of time.

Long-reining has proven to have many benefits in comparison to other training methods.

Specific benefits:

- Constant contact can be maintained on both long reins.
- The suppleness of the horse's position and contact can be continuously checked by the trainer.
- The haunches can be evenly activated.
- Forward movement can easily be controlled and maintained (the horse will continuously pull forward).
- Uneven steps (loss of rhythm) can easily be corrected by moving forward.
- Building tension can immediately be resolved by moving the horse onto a circle.
- The passage can easily be developed by walking with the horse in a brisk tempo.
- The horse is able to move with more lightness and cadence without the rider on his back.
- The transition between piaffe and passage can be fluid.
- The work can take place without an arena wall or kickboard.

Sometimes, long-reining may be the **only way** to develop piaffe and passage.

Important!
In order to collaborate harmoniously with the horse, the trainer needs to be knowledgeable, sensitive, and skillful, and must have a high level of empathy.

After concluding work on the long reins, allow the horse to cool down in a long-and-low frame. This may require a change of the height at which the long reins attach.

Once a horse is able to perform a piaffe with cadence, and an elevated and expressive passage, as well as fluid transitions, one of the main goals of dressage training has been reached. These elegant movements are especially indicative of the horse's gains in carrying power and springiness.

Piaffe and passage are proof that the trainer is in fact able to cultivate the horse's movements, and that the gaits have become more elastic, beautiful. and expressive. As **Xenophon** said: **"The horse appears proud."**

In the end, you cannot expect miracles from long-reining. Success will depend on the skill and experience of the trainer. Long reins can only support the rider or driver in reaching the highest possible level of harmony and performance if the trainer is able to develop horses systematically, following the Training Scale in small learning units.

The author demonstrates an expressive piaffe with Amant, with minimal aids and absolute willingness. A surcingle is not necessary. Naturally, the bend in the haunches and the elevation are balanced and in perfect relation.

15 Problems and Solutions—33 of the Most Common Questions and Situations

What to Do If...

. . . the horse falls out over his shoulder?

- Give more with the inside hand.
- Work on a circle with an outer boundary.
- Change the attachment of the inside long rein: hand—mouth—surcingle.
- Change direction often.

. . . the horse comes into the circle and is positioned to the outside?

- Point the whip toward the shoulder to move the horse out, while positioning him to the inside with your inside hand.
- Put the horse into the correct frame with "guarding" long rein aids.

. . . the horse alternately pushes out and falls in?

- Attach the long reins as in the first chapter: hand—mouth—surcingle.
- Ask the horse to go forward.
- Use a double-longeing circle.
- Long-rein toward the outside.

. . . the horse moves on two tracks?

- If the hindquarters are coming in, make sure the outside long rein is not too tight.
- If the horse moves the hindquarters out, make sure the outside long rein is not too loose.

. . . the long rein slides under the tail and gets stuck?

- Immediately loosen the outside long rein.
- Wait until the horse lets go of the long rein.
- Attach the long reins further down on the surcingle.

. . . the long rein slides across the back?

- Attach the long reins further down on the surcingle.
- Try using long reins with mechanical rollers (to redirect the reins—see p. 31).

. . . the horse kicks out above the long reins?

- Stay calm.
- Transition to a halt.
- Have an assistant hold the horse; reorganize the long reins and then continue with the work.

. . . the horse is not on the bit?

- Encourage the horse to "give" by alternating forward-driving and shortening aids.
- Check the height at which the long reins attach.

. . . the horse is on the bit but going on the forehand?

- Activate the haunches.
- Try attaching the long reins higher.

. . . the horse is short in the neck?

- Be lighter in the contact (let his nose reach forward).
- Apply more forward-driving aids.
- Attach the long reins higher (or try using long reins with mechanical rollers).
- Reduce friction at the surcingle.
- Use a lighter set of long reins.

. . . the horse doesn't react to the whip?

- Use a longer whip.
- Use the whip more deliberately.
- Have an assistant take the whip.

. . . the horse comes toward the trainer?

- Lead with the outside long rein.
- Use the whip to help the horse learn to respect it.

. . . the horse is overactive to the whip and bolts?

- Start out without a whip.
- Use a short whip.

- Use extreme caution in the beginning (don't pick up the whip or point it, just hold it under your arm) and when changing direction.

. . . the horse doesn't accept the aids for transitions between the gaits?

- Warm the horse up more thoroughly.
- Improve the coordination of the aids (voice, long reins, whip).
- Practice transitions in the same spot using the same aids.

. . . the horse is crooked in the poll?

- Check the horse's teeth.
- Develop more stretch, so the horse is long and low.
- Compare the height at which the long reins attach on each side.
- Warm the horse up more thoroughly.
- Change direction often.

. . . the horse is heavy on the bit?

- Use efficient forward-driving aids.
- Use shortening aids only briefly.
- Take away the support of the long reins by "giving."

. . . the horse does not accept the aids for the halt?

- Practice the halt from the walk.
- Practice the trot-to-halt transition in the same place every time.
- Use the same aids each time.
- Prepare for the halt well with half-halts.

. . . the horse gets short in the neck during downward transitions?

- Use more voice than long rein for the transitions.
- "Give" more.

. . . the canter depart from the walk is not uphill?

- First, practice canter departs from the trot in the same spot.
- Then put the horse securely on the aids in the walk.
- Then attempt a canter depart in the same spot.

. . . the horse gets on the forehand during the transition from canter to walk, or can only transition through the trot to the walk?

- First, collect the canter by decreasing the size of a circle.
- Immediately "give" with the long reins after the downward transition.

. . . the transitions are "sticky"?

- Sensitize the horse.
- Don't get stuck in the half-halt; give quickly.
- Use voice and whip to move the horse forward.

. . . the horse gets tangled up in the long reins?

- Stay calm (often, the horse will untangle himself).
- Have an assistant hold the horse; remove the long reins, untangle them, and reattach them, and then continue the work.

. . . the horse regresses after being long-reined?

- Reflect on the long-reining technique.
- Consider whether you have enough experience with the long reins; perhaps you are not yet qualified to advance the horse's training.

. . . the horse gets nervous or strong?

- Warm the horse up more thoroughly.
- Build trust.
- Take a few steps back in training.

. . . the horse overreacts to the groundwork whip?

- Familiarize the horse with the whip while standing still.
- Warm the horse up more thoroughly.
- Build trust.
- Take a few steps back in training.

. . . the horse loses rhythm in the walk?

- Give more with the long reins.
- Walk briskly yourself.
- Attach the long reins lower on the surcingle.

. . . the horse tries to evade to the inside?

- Let the horse be led by an assistant.
- Carry the whip on the inside.
- Don't let tension rise.
- Ask an assistant for help.

. . . the horse gets short in the neck?

- Attach the long reins higher on the surcingle.
- Be lighter with your hands; give more with the long reins.

. . . the horse is not on the bit?

- Attach the long reins lower on the surcingle.

. . . the horse doesn't stand still at the halt?

- Ask an assistant to calm the horse.
- Let the horse stand longer, and wait.

. . . the horse shows resistance when asked to back up?

- Ask an assistant for help.

. . . the horse loses the diagonal footfall pattern in the piaffe?

- Think more forward during this exercise.
- Don't use the groundwork whip against the movement.

. . . the horse doesn't transition to the trot and is dull?

- Shorten the warm-up (preserve the horse's energy).
- Deliberately touch the whip to specific reflex points, and simultaneously use energetic voice commands.
- Minimize your aids over time.
- Only work forward, use short trot sequences, and don't ask for collection.

Index

Page numbers in *italics* indicate illustrations.